STUDENT UNIT

89

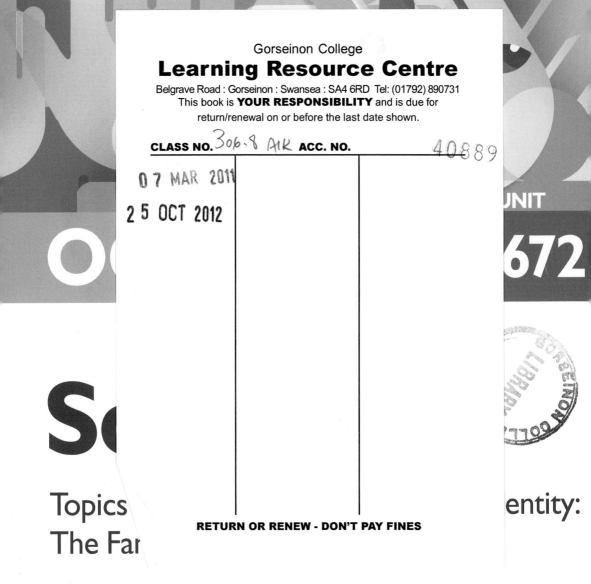

UNIT

672

O

S

Topics   entity:
The Far

Dave Aiken

Series Editor: Steve Chapman

Thanks to Maggie for all her love and support. In loving memory of Joe Bane, father of Maggie and Kathy, who died 31 December 2007.

Philip Allan Updates, an imprint of Hodder Education, an Hachette UK Company, Market Place, Deddington, Oxfordshire OX15 0SE

Orders
Bookpoint Ltd, 130 Milton Park, Abingdon, Oxfordshire, OX14 4SB
tel: 01235 827720
fax: 01235 400454
e-mail: uk.orders@bookpoint.co.uk
Lines are open 9.00 a.m.–5.00 p.m., Monday to Saturday, with a 24-hour message answering service. You can also order through the Philip Allan Updates website: www.philipallan.co.uk

© Philip Allan Updates 2008

ISBN 978-0-340-96802-4

First printed 2008

Impression number 5   4   3   2
Year 2013 2012 2011 2010 2009

This guide has been written specifically to support students preparing for the OCR AS Sociology Unit G672 examination. The content has been neither approved nor endorsed by OCR and remains the sole responsibility of the author.

Typeset by Phoenix Photosetting, Chatham, Kent
Printed by MPG Books, Bodmin

P01239

40889

Sociology

Contents

Introduction

■ ■ ■

Content Guidance

40889

■ ■ ■

Questions and Answers

Introduction

About this guide

This unit guide is for students following the OCR AS Sociology course. It deals with the topic The Family, which is an option in Unit G672 **Topics in Socialisation, Culture and Identity**. The family is a central institution of socialisation and social reproduction because of its traditional role as the site in which children are reared. It plays an important role in mediating the relationship between the individual, groups and society. This option therefore builds on Unit G671: **Exploring Socialisation, Culture and Identity**.

There are three sections to this guide:
- **Introduction** — provides advice on how to use this unit guide, an explanation of the skills required in AS Sociology and suggestions for effective revision. It concludes with guidance on how to succeed in the unit test.
- **Content Guidance** — provides an outline of what is included in the specification for the topic 'The Family'. It is designed to make you aware of what you should know before the unit test.
- **Questions and Answers** — this provides mock exam questions on The Family for you to try, together with some sample answers at grade-A and grade-C level. Examiner's comments on how the marks are awarded are included.

How to use the guide

To use this guide to your best advantage, you should refer to the Introduction and Content Guidance sections from the beginning of your study of The Family. However, in order to get full advantage from the Questions and Answers section, you would be advised to wait until you have completed your study of the topic, as the questions are wide-ranging. When you are ready to use this section, you should take each question in turn, study it carefully, and either write a full answer yourself or, at the very least, answer part (a) fully and write a plan for part (b). When you have done this, study the grade-A candidate's answer and compare it with your own, paying close attention to the examiner's comments. You could also look at the grade-C answers and, using the examiner's comments as a guide, work out how to rewrite them to gain higher marks.

These tasks are quite intensive and time-consuming, and you are advised not to try to tackle all the questions at once or in a short space of time. It is better to focus on one at a time and spread the workload over several weeks — you can always find some time to do this, even while studying another topic. In addition to using the questions to consolidate your own knowledge and develop your exam skills, you should use at least some of the questions as revision practice — even just reading through the grade-A candidates' answers should provide you with useful revision material.

The AS specification

The aims of the OCR AS Sociology specification are to encourage candidates to:
- acquire knowledge and a critical understanding of contemporary social processes and social changes
- appreciate the significance of theoretical and conceptual issues in sociological debate
- understand and evaluate sociological methodology and a range of research methods through active involvement in the research process
- develop skills that enable individuals to focus on their personal identity, roles and responsibilities within society
- develop a lifelong interest in social issues

Examinable skills

There are two main examinable skills or **assessment objectives** in the AS specifica-tions.

Assessment objective 1

Assessment objective 1 (AO1) is **knowledge and understanding**, which accounts for 53% of the AS marks on offer. After studying this specification you should be able to demonstrate knowledge and understanding of sociological concepts, methods and different types of evidence, especially empirical studies. In some units there is a need to demonstrate an introductory knowledge of theory and especially the concepts that underpin it. You will need to show how concepts, evidence and methods are inter-linked and how they relate to both social life and social problems in a clear and effective manner.

It is important that your acquisition of knowledge goes beyond learning by rote. You also need to demonstrate understanding. Generally, this is displayed by learning and using knowledge which is appropriate and relevant to the question set. A good way of doing this is to ask yourself the following questions:
- Do I know the main arguments in the area I am studying?
- Do I know the main sociologists who have contributed to debate in this area?
- Do I understand the concepts used by these sociologists?
- Do I know the empirical studies and data that can be used as evidence to support or undermine particular sociological arguments?

It is important to stress here that the exam board is not expecting or requiring an advanced understanding of sociological theory. Rather, at this level, the examiners are looking for you to be 'conceptually confident', meaning that they want you to demon-strate that you understand important concepts and are able to apply these when constructing a sociological argument. It is also a good idea to know some sociological studies because these often count as evidence in support of a particular view.

Examiners also take account of your ability to communicate knowledge and under-standing in a clear and effective manner, so you need to make sure that you express your ideas concisely and unambiguously. Specialist vocabulary should be used appropriately. Text should be legible and spelling, punctuation and grammar accurate so that meaning is clear.

Assessment objective 2 (AO2)

Assessment objective 2 is **analysis, evaluation and application**. This assessment objective makes up the other 47% of marks available.

For the purposes of the unit mark scheme, it is divided into two parts:
- AO2(a): interpretation and application
- AO2(b): evaluation and analysis

Interpretation and application requires accurate interpretation of patterns and/or trends and/or research data for both sides of the argument presented. This essentially involves showing the ability to consider different types of evidence and data. It also involves the ability to make sense of quantitative and qualitative data — that is, to work out what such data tell us and/or to put this interpretation into your own words. You then need to be able to apply it to the particular context being discussed. This involves linking the evidence to specific sociological arguments. It is useful to ask yourself the following questions when working out whether you have acquired this skill:
- What evidence in the form of studies, concepts and so on is relevant when addressing a particular debate?
- Can I distinguish between facts and opinions?
- Am I capable of identifying patterns and trends in sociological data and uncovering hidden meanings?
- Am I addressing the question throughout the response?
- Have I applied contemporary issues and debates to the question?
- What evidence in the form of sociological studies and statistical data can I use to support or criticise particular arguments?
- Am I staying focused and applying relevant material, not just 'what I know', which may not serve any purpose and merely waste time?

Evaluation and analysis normally involves assessing the usefulness and validity of particular sociological arguments and available evidence and data or critically examining the reliability of the methods used to collect that evidence. The skill of evaluation is an important one, and should be applied to all the material you come across during your study of the topic. It is useful to ask yourself the following questions when practising this skill:
- How many sides to the debate can be identified in this area?
- How was the evidence gathered?
- Can the evidence be checked?
- Is there any other evidence relating to this?
- Is the research relevant to contemporary society?

- Who does not agree with this view and why?
- Which evidence and arguments are most convincing and why?
- What have sociologists and social commentators got to gain from saying what they say?
- Are class, gender and ethnicity taken into account?

In perhaps more practical terms, it means that whenever you are introduced to a sociological perspective or study, you should find and learn at least two criticisms that have been made of it. You should also note, of course, which group or person has made these criticisms, as this is an important piece of information.

Study skills and revision strategies

Good preparation for revision actually starts the minute you begin to study sociology.

Keeping a sociology folder

One of the most important revision aids that you will have is your sociology folder, so it is important that you keep this in good order. Essentially, it should be divided into topic areas. It should contain all your class notes, handouts, notes you have made from textbooks, class and homework exercises and all your marked and returned work. If you are not by nature a neat and tidy person, you may find that you have to rewrite notes you make in class into a legible and coherent form before putting them in your folder. Be warned, though — this is something you should do straight away, as after only a few days you will have forgotten things.

If you keep a good folder throughout your course, reading through this will form a major part of your revision. In addition, you will need to re-read the relevant parts of your textbooks.

Summarising concepts and studies

You should always write down the definition of a concept when you first come across it — you will find it helpful to use a separate part of your folder for this purpose.

In addition, it is also very useful to make a brief summary of research studies, particularly those not found within your textbook. Remember to include the title, author(s) and, most importantly, the date, along with your summary of the method(s) used and the main findings. Again, these should be kept in a section in your sociology folder, or you may wish to use a set of index cards for this purpose.

Writing and re-reading essays

Your own work forms an important revision resource. Go back over your essays and exam answers, read your teacher's comments, and use these to see whether you can re-do any pieces that did not score particularly good marks.

Another important aspect of revision is to practise writing answers within the appropriate time limit. Make sure you have sufficient time not only to complete all the parts of the question, but also to reread your answer in order to correct any silly mistakes that may have crept in while working under pressure.

Reinforcing your understanding

Finally, you need to ensure that you have retained a thorough understanding of a range of appropriate concepts and studies. Again, this planned and comprehensive revision is not something that can be done the night before the exam — you should start at least a couple of weeks before the exam, and revise in concentrated bursts of time. People differ in this respect, but it is seldom a good idea to spend more than 2 hours at a time on revision and, for most people, two or three stints of an hour at a time spread out over a day or two will be more productive than a 2- or 3-hour session, particularly late at night.

The unit test

The Family is one of four options in unit G672 (which also includes Health, Religion and Youth). The unit examination will contain a choice of **two** two-part structured questions in each topic. You are required to answer any two questions. You may choose to answer both questions in The Family or another topic or two questions from different topics. In any case, you have to answer parts (a) and (b) of the same question each time. The unit as a whole is worth 50% of the AS mark and 25% of the full A-level. Each structured question totals 50 marks, composed of 17 marks in part(a) for AO1 (knowledge and understanding), and in part (b) 10 marks for AO1 (knowledge and understanding), 13 marks for AO2(a) (interpretation and application) and 10 marks for AO2(b) (evaluation and analysis). The total mark allocation for the paper is therefore 100 marks for both questions answered over 1 hour 30 minutes.

Do not be put off by the mark allocations. A general rule of thumb is that 1 mark is equivalent to a little over 1 minute of writing. Therefore, you should spend 17 minutes on part (a) and 33 minutes on part (b) in each of the two questions, including reading and checking time.

Part (a) questions always take the same basic form and use consistent command words throughout the topics examined. The question will always use the command phrase **'Identify and explain two...'** and will instruct you to focus on **two** things related to key features of family life that underpin this unit. In the family topic, for example, part (a) questions have asked candidates to:

- Identify and explain **two** recent demographic changes and the ways in which they have affected family life.
- Identify and explain **two** reasons for the growth in lone-parent households.
- Identify and explain **two** ways in which families differ from households.
- Identify and explain **two** ways in which family life may be influenced by changing work patterns.

It is therefore essential when responding to this question that you make sure you clearly distinguish between two things in your identification and, moreover, that you explain their meaning, perhaps adding clarity to your explanation by using illustration and example. However, don't get carried away with your response. Remember that you are only required to demonstrate 'knowledge and understanding' for this part of the question. No marks will be awarded for sustained criticism or analysis. You just need to show that you know about two features related to family life and can illustrate this knowledge appropriately. You should spend approximately 15 minutes on your response and aim for two concise paragraphs.

Part (b) questions require a more developed and evaluative response using sociological evidence to back it up. This may take the form of empirical evidence such as statistics or substantive examples and/or sociological studies and/or theory. The part (b) question is worth 33 marks. The question will always use the command phrase **'Outline and evaluate the view...'** and will be followed by a statement — usually controversial — relating to an aspect of family life. For example:
- Outline and evaluate the view that changes in women's role in society have had a major impact upon family life.
- Outline and evaluate the view that families are now so diverse that the idea of the 'normal' nuclear family no longer applies.

The command 'evaluate' requires you to outline or describe the issues and evidence relating to the view presented and to weigh up their relative relevance and validity. You must be aware of some criticisms too; do not simply present a position in support of the view. Be prepared also to challenge it. Each question for part (b) is essentially an essay question and you should aim for approximately two sides of A4. Spend about 30 minutes on your response to each of the part (b) questions you attempt.

Content
Guidance

This section is intended to show you the major issues and themes covered in The Family in the OCR specification. However, it is not an exhaustive or comprehensive list of the concepts, issues and sociological studies that you could use to answer questions on this topic. Rather, it is an outline guide that should give you a good idea of the key concepts that are essential to know and some issues and sociological studies that are worth further investigation. You should be able to access additional useful information from your teacher, the textbook you are using and past copies of *Sociology Review*.

Introduction

The content of The Family topic falls into four main areas, which, in turn, are further subdivided.

- key concepts and key trends within the family
- the role of the family in society
- family diversity
- roles, responsibilities and relationships within the family

Content	Guidance
1 Key concepts and key trends within the family	

(i) Key concepts:
  • nuclear families
  • extended families
  • households
	This is an introduction to the family. Stress key definitions, key structural trends and the importance of extended family networks in contemporary society.

(ii) Trends in families and households:
  • family size
  • marriage
  • divorce
  • cohabitation
  • single-parent families
  • single-person households
	Trends over the past 30 years, longer only if they illustrate a significant point (e.g. Divorce Reform Acts).

2 The role of the family in society	
Functionalism	Functionalist views of the role of the family and an evaluation of the views. Include views on the domestic division of labour. Stress positive role of nuclear family.
Marxism	Marxist views of the family and evaluation of the views. Stress conflict and change.
3 Family diversity	
Different types of family diversity: • lone-parent families • beanpole families • re-constituted families • cultural diversity • class diversity • sexual diversity	The key issue to explore is the range and extent of diversity in contemporary family life.
Contemporary views of family diversity: • postmodern • New Right	Contemporary views of family diversity, which should include postmodernism and New Right ideas. New Labour views can be referred to. Include evaluation of each.

4 Roles, responsibilities and relationships within the family	
Roles, responsibilities and relationships in family life, including: • between men and women • between children and parents	The key issues are the relationship between men and women in family life, and between children and parents. Links should be made to current government policy.
Sociological explanations: • functionalist • Marxist • feminist explanations (liberal, Marxist, radical)	A range of theories/explanations should be covered with an evaluation of each. You could include reference to the dark side of family life as a criticism of functionalism.
Demographic changes, including: • ageing population • family size	Demographic changes and the impact on family life. Changes such as an ageing population, the importance of carers, smaller family size, and reliance on extended kin could be considered.

The OCR AS topic The Family is designed to give you a good understanding of the relationship between individuals, the family and wider social structures. In particular, it aims to examine influences such as gender, social class, ethnicity and religion on people's experience of family life and on family organisation, as well as the relationship of the family to other agencies and the significance of social policy for family life. The Family topic has particular relevance for the synoptic Unit G674 in A2 (*Exploring Social Inequality and Difference*), where issues of family lifestyle, consumption, work and income, family structures and ethnic diversity all impact upon life chances, poverty and inequality. So, A2 students preparing for the synoptic test may also benefit from revisiting aspects of The Family topic and students intending to progress to A2 should annotate their notes in some way to highlight the synoptic links.

For the purposes of guidance, each of the four subsections that follow relates to the content headings from the specification outlined above.

Key concepts and key trends within the family

Family concepts and definitions

A **family** is a group of people who are united by blood, marriage or adoption. Members are usually bound by legal, moral and economic rights and duties and consequently have distinct obligations to one another. In addition, there are normally emotional ties. Members also tend to perform particular roles in line with social norms (e.g.

husband, wife, son, daughter etc.). The nucleus of the family — father, mother and children — may share common residence but other extended family members may live elsewhere. **Kinship** involves interaction between groups of family members (i.e. kin) expressed in various mutual forms of emotional, economic and social support.

The concept of a **household** refers to a group of people who share common residence. A family that shares a common residence is a household. However, those who make up a household need not be necessarily related — a group of students who share a house constitute a household.

Families take many diverse structural forms but the type of family discussed most by sociologists has been the **nuclear family**, which consists of parents and their children. It was assumed for many years in modern Britain that a nuclear family was the ideal type of family that people should attempt to achieve. It was assumed that this nuclear family should have the following characteristics:
- Its members should be biologically related.
- It should be based upon heterosexual romantic love.
- It should be based upon marriage.
- There should be a sexual division of labour based on natural differences — women should be primarily responsible for childcare while men should be the breadwinner and head of household.

However, the latter part of the twentieth century saw women moving into paid work in large numbers and men increasing their participation in housework and childcare. Despite its prominence in discussions of family life, this nuclear family only represents 39% of family forms in Britain.

Key trends in family life

The shift from extended families

Fifty years ago it was believed that family life, especially working-class family life, was characterised by the **classical extended family**.

This classical extended family comprised mutually dependent family members, either living together or geographically close. It may have been **vertically extended** (comprised of more than one generation of mutually dependent members such as children, parents and grandparents), and/or **horizontally extended** (involving the mutual dependency and interaction of relatives within the same generation, for example aunts, uncles, cousins, married siblings etc.). In such families, regular — often daily — contact between family members was maintained, compared with the more isolated **nuclear family,** which is thought to maintain less regular contact with wider kin.

However, sociologists such as Wilmott and Young have argued that over the past 50 years, this extended unit has gradually been replaced by the isolated nuclear family (which is less likely to maintain regular contact with kin) for a number of reasons.
- Full employment in the 1950s led to rises in pay and living standards, and consequently people were less dependent on other family members for economic supports.

- Full employment led to an expansion in the number of jobs available, which meant that sons did not necessarily have to follow fathers into the same jobs.
- The expansion of secondary education meant that working-class children often experienced upward social mobility into white collar, managerial and professional jobs.
- Full employment led to geographical mobility — people moved away from areas in which their families had traditionally lived in order to better themselves.
- The welfare state, and particularly the benefits system, reduced the need for an extended family mutual support system.

Evaluation

- The concept of 'contact' with regard to nuclear families depends on how it is being measured. While it is true that members of some families do not have a great deal of face-to-face contact with kin, mainly because of geographical distance, links may be maintained in other ways, for example by telephone, e-mails, and so on. It may therefore be unwise to suggest that nuclear families are isolated from kin.
- Litwak suggests that nuclear families should be referred to as **modified extended families** because family life in the UK today is often made up of a coalition of nuclear families who are partially dependent on each other and who exchange significant services with each other. However, unlike the classical extended family, these family relationships are not bound together economically or geographically; members have considerable autonomy, but they are not cut off or as remote as is suggested by the notion of the isolated nuclear family.
- Alternatively, Peter Willmott notes the emergence of a **dispersed extended family**. Members live some distance apart but keep in fairly regular contact, perhaps once a week by car, telephone and public transport. While not dependent on each other, they do feel a family obligation or duty to help each other occasionally if a crisis occurs.
- However, the classical extended family is still very much in evidence in some areas. Janet Foster in her study *Villains* (1991) showed how the lives of working-class people and their children in London's East End were still dominated by the values and traditions of extended kin such as parents and grandparents who lived nearby. Also, there is evidence that many ethnic minority communities, particularly Asian communities, have horizontal extended family structures at their heart.

The rise of lone-parent families

There has been a significant growth in the number and percentage of families headed by single or 'lone' parents (the overwhelming majority of whom are women). The **lone-parent family** unit now comprises almost one in four of all families with dependent children.

There are a number of reasons offered for the growth in lone-parent families:

- The increased incidence of separation and divorce.
- The feminisation of the economy and workplace, which has increased the economic choices available to females (compared with 50 years ago). There are now more opportunities for women to enjoy careers and to be economically

independent of men. There is some evidence that these women are choosing to have children in their mid- to late thirties but are less likely to do this in a conventional relationship (i.e. they choose to bring up children alone).

- Helen Wilkinson argues that a radical change — which she terms a 'genderquake' — has occurred and consequently the idea of bringing up children alone is no longer unthinkable to modern women.
- New Right sociologists have argued that a breakdown in traditional family and moral values is occurring and that the high divorce rate and the high rate of teenage pregnancy in the UK are symbolic of this.
- New Right sociologists suggest that the availability of welfare benefits has also encouraged female members of a so-called underclass (see page 22) to choose to have children rather than go to work and earn a living.
- Changing religious and social values, especially the decline in religious belief among the majority of the population, mean that single mothers are less likely to be stigmatised and labelled as deviant.

New Right thinkers such as Murray (1994) suggest that children of single parents suffer from lower educational achievement and are more likely to become delinquent.

Evaluation

- Only 3% of single parents are teenagers.
- The average age of a single mother is 34; these are mainly divorced women.
- Despite welfare benefits, the economic situation of single parenthood offers little financial incentive to become pregnant as the New Right suggest. Seventeen percent of those officially defined as poor are single parents.
- Single parenthood can be a realistic strategy in poor areas where fathers cannot offer economic support due to unemployment or low wages.
- Home Office reports have found no difference in the crime rates between youngsters from single- and two-parent families.

Other trends

Marriage and cohabitation

There has been a fall in the marriage rate, and a growth in **cohabitation** over the last 30 years. Although marriage is still the usual form of partnership between men and women, the number of marriages has declined substantially since a peak in 1970. Currently, roughly a quarter of all non-married men and women between the ages of 16 and 59 are cohabiting at any one time. Cohabitation is, of course, often followed by marriage and thus the age of first marriage is increasing. In 1971 the average age of first marriage was 22 for women and 24 for men. By 2001 this had increased to 28.4 and 30.6 for women and men respectively.

Wilkinson (1994) has noted that female attitudes to marriage have undergone a 'genderquake', whereby many middle-class young women are weighing up the relative advantages of family life against the opportunities offered by education and an increasingly feminised workplace and so are opting out of marriage and motherhood altogether.

Divorce

We have seen an increase in the **divorce rate** following various legal changes, partic-ularly the implementation in 1971 of the Divorce Law Reform Act. The increase in the number of divorces appears to have leveled off in recent years, partly reflecting the fall in the number of marriages and the possibility that increased cohabitation may mean that cohabitees who marry may be better suited, because they have got to know each other's strengths and limitations before marriage.

The reasons for the rise in divorce up to the mid-1980s include the following.

- Legal changes made it easier for divorces to be granted (the Divorce Reform Act only required 2 years' legal separation before a divorce was granted, compared with the previous expensive and lengthy system, which involved proving that the husband or wife was 'guilty' of a matrimonial offence such as adultery).
- Changing social attitudes (partly as a result of the growing incidence of divorce) made marital breakdown more socially acceptable.
- There were signs from the 1980s onwards that people expected more from marriage than previous generations, especially women. Thornes and Collard (1992) showed that women expect more from marriage than men and so are more easily dissatisfied.
- Feminist ideas, particularly the idea that women have a right to personal happi-ness and fulfilment within marriage, have probably contributed to the fact that women are the main petitioners for divorce — seven of every ten divorce decrees are granted to women.
- The declining influence of the Christian church has meant that moral or religious opposition to divorce has been relatively weak.
- Kin are increasingly isolated from a supportive kinship network whose members in previous generations might have encouraged couples to work through their marital problems.
- There is evidence that modern society is more stressful because of long hours spent at work and financial pressures.

Growth of single-person households

The number of people living alone has tripled since 1960, currently comprising almost 30% of all households. Almost half of these one-person households consist of a person under pensionable age. There are a variety of reasons for this particular trend, some of which are mentioned below:

- The increased economic independence of women (women are no longer 'a husband away from poverty').
- The growth of **young singletons** — young people who may be in a relationship but who choose to live alone.
- The rise in the number of divorced or separated people who have not formed another co-residential partnership.
- The increase in **life expectancy** has added to the number of elderly widowed people living alone.

Many argue, in particular the New Right, that increases in divorce, the decline in the **marriage rate** and the growth of cohabitation and single-person households indicate a decline in family life.

Evaluation

Abbott and Wallace (1992) reinterpret family statistics to demonstrate the continuing stability of the family. They show that:

- Six out of ten couples stay together until one of them dies.
- Seven out of ten children are born to parents who live together, three quarters of whom are married.
- Only one in five children experience parental divorce by the age of 16.
- 78% of British children under 16 live with both natural parents who are legally married.

Changes in family lifestyle

There has been a rise in **dual career** or **dual income families**, who can enjoy a more affluent lifestyle, indulge in more conspicuous consumption and leisure activities such as a new car or family holiday abroad, compared to the single-earner households of the past.

There has also been an increase in the number of **'empty-nest' families**, as children grow up and leave the family while the parents are still relatively young. This is coupled to the rise in life expectancy. However, in parts of the country where living and housing costs are high, there has been an increasing trend for young people either to continue living with their parents for the duration of their studies or to return to the family home after higher education.

Key concepts

family; kinship; household; nuclear family; classical extended family; isolated nuclear family; extended family; lone-parent families; cohabitation; divorce rate; young singletons; life expectancy; marriage rate; dual income families; 'empty nest' families

The role of the family in society

The family has been perceived in both positive and negative terms by sociologists.

Functionalist perspectives

Functionalists see the family as a beneficial institution which has evolved to meet the needs of modern industrial society.

- Parsons (1955) argues that specialised agencies took over many family functions after industrialisation (education, health and economic production). According to Parsons, the family is therefore left with only two basic and irreducible functions: (a) the primary socialisation of children (i.e. the transmission of basic human behaviour patterns), and (b) the stabilisation of adult personality (for example, the married couple keep each other emotionally and mentally balanced and therefore able to cope with the stresses of modern living).

- The nuclear family is a vital agency of **primary socialisation** because it transmits culture from one generation to another, so ensuring the reproduction of society and social order. **Secondary socialisation** involves more complex elements of human social behaviour developed through socialising agents beyond infancy and the family.
- Parsons argues that the family acts as a personality factory, producing children whose behaviour is shaped by key societal values such as individualism and achievement.
- Parsons argues that individuals also benefit from the family because parents gain stability and satisfaction from having children and are able to sustain each other emotionally, physically and sexually. This latter function has been called the **warm bath theory**, in that the family provides the means to relax and relieve the frustrations of modern living.
- However, Fletcher (1966) disagrees with Parsons and argues that the family continues to fulfil health, educational and welfare functions hand-in-hand with the state.

Some functionalist and New Right sociologists argue that socialisation in modern society is becoming less effective because of trends such as increasing divorce and the lack of a father in many one-parent families. Furthermore, they argue that this is contributing to social problems such as increased delinquency and educational under-achievement.

Evaluation

- The functionalist perspective overestimates the success of the socialisation process, as indicated by the existence of problems such as child abuse, youth suicide, eating disorders etc.
- So-called common values transmitted through the family may be the values of dominant social groups.
- Functionalism presents an **over-socialised view** of children. For example, children may negotiate socialisation with parents and parents themselves may be socialised into particular ways of thinking or behaviour by their children.
- Functionalism presents socialisation as a universal homogeneous experience and consequently neglects differences due to wealth, social class, ethnicity, religion etc.
- There is no universal agreement on how socialisation should occur, as indicated by the debate about smacking children.
- There is convincing evidence from Phoenix (1995) and Cashmore (1985) that one-parent families can successfully socialise children and the absence of a father does not significantly damage children.

Some functionalist sociologists, for example Leach (1967), are critical of the nuclear family. He argues that it is too intense and inward-looking and, like an overloaded electrical circuit or pressure cooker, has the potential to explode.

Marxism

Marxists such as Zaretsky (1976) argue that the nuclear family benefits capitalism more than other forms because it can be used as an **ideological apparatus** to promote capitalist interests. For example, it is targeted as a unit of consumption by advertisers and consequently buys many more consumer items than other family forms. Other Marxists note that in families, children learn to submit to parental authority and discipline and therefore they acquire the appropriate attitudes to hierarchy (passive acceptance, obedience etc.) required of the capitalist division of labour in the workplace. Furthermore, in industrial societies, the family helps to service and maintain the economic system by reproducing the future workforce and promoting a positive work ethic. It also cushions the effects of capitalism by providing opportunities for satisfaction no longer available through work.

Feminism

Many feminists see the family as oppressive for women because it has traditionally confined them either to the home or to subordinate positions in society. It is expected socially that they should be mainly responsible for the care of the young and elderly. These domestic or family roles inhibit their wider social and economic opportunities. In terms of the wider society, the role of the family is seen as one supportive of both **patriarchy** (male dominance of social institutions and decision-making) and capitalism.

> **Key concepts**
>
> primary socialisation; secondary socialisation; warm bath theory; over-socialised view; ideological apparatus; patriarchy

Family diversity

Sociologists note that there are many distinctive forms of family existing today. However, the idea that one particular type of family should be the preferred model has been dominant both in popular culture and functionalist and New Right thinking for over a century. Such thinking is referred to as the **ideology of familism**, which promotes certain values regarding family life over others (for example, it is often assumed without question that the primary care-giver should be the female while the male should be the breadwinner, or that children need both parents to ensure that they are properly brought up and disciplined).

Sociological discussion of these issues is referred to as the **family values debate**. This debate is particularly interested in the fact that government social policy still appears actively to promote the two-parent nuclear family, while other social policies are seen to undermine it. Feminists, for example, believe that family social policies reflect an ideological view that actively tries to promote a particular type of family structure, namely that of the nuclear family, at the expense of women and to the benefit of men in society.

On the other hand, New Right sociologists argue that certain social policies (for example, providing welfare benefits for single mothers, and making divorce easier) undermine the traditional family structure and contribute to 'social problems'. They accuse the government of being a **nanny state**, creating welfare dependency and disincentives to work as well as discouraging individual responsibility. This, they argue, has created an **underclass** unable and unwilling to work for a living.

Examples of family diversity

Single-parent families

This type of family involves a lone parent, usually a divorced woman. Such families often involve close ties with wider kin, especially grandparents.

Beanpole families

Historically, families have usually contained a larger number of children than parents, resulting in family trees that looked like pyramids. In recent years, especially in Britain and the USA, the number of children per generation has gone down steadily and life span has increased. This has led to a new shape of family tree that some researchers have likened to a beanpole — tall and thin, with few people in each generation.

Julia Brannen argues that people are having smaller families due to divorce and women pursuing careers, and as a result, we are less likely to experience **horizontal intragenerational ties** (we have fewer aunts, uncles and cousins). However, Brannen argues that we are now more likely to experience **vertical intergenerational ties** (closer ties with grandparents and great-grandparents) because of increased life expectancy.

Brannen argues that the **pivot generation** (the one sandwiched between older and younger family generations) provides for the needs of both elderly parents and grand-children. For example, 20% of people in their fifties and sixties currently care for an elderly person, while 10% care for both an elderly person and a grandchild. Such services are based on the assumption of **reciprocity** (the provision of babysitting services is repaid by the assumption that daughters will assist their mothers in their old age).

Reconstituted or 'step' families

There has been a growth in **reconstituted** or 'step' families following divorce and remarriage. More than two in five of all marriages involve the remarriage of at least one partner, and a growing number of children live with a step-parent. Monogamy (one partner for life) is being replaced by serial monogamy — a series of long-term relationships which result in cohabitation/marriage and children. Each relationship eventually breaks down and is in time replaced by another, resulting in remarriage and a reconstituted family.

Evaluation

- Reconstituted families — especially the children in them — are likely to have close ties with the families of previous partners. Children may be pulled in two directions and have tense relationships with their step-parents.
- Relationships may be further complicated when parents decide to have children of their own.
- Many reconstituted families are able to develop harmonious relationships, especially where ex-partners are also happy in new relationships, and previous resentments eventually subside.

Other dimensions of diversity

There exist important differences in family and household structures based on family life cycle, class, age, ethnicity, sexuality and region.

Life-cycle diversity

Family life is not experienced as a continuous fixed pattern of relationships. Each stage of a family's life cycle differs from the one before. Young couples with children, for example, have different family experiences compared with middle-aged couples whose children have left home.

Cohort diversity

Certain groups of families may face particular circumstances not experienced by others. For example, in periods of high unemployment, young people may remain dependent upon their parents for a greater period of time. Families established during the economic booms of the 1960s and 1980s also had much more economic security than those who struggled through the recessions of the 1970s and 1990s.

Cultural diversity

This can be found between various **ethnic groups**. There are differences in the lifestyles of families with different ethnic origins and religious beliefs. Berthoud (2000) found that only 39% of British-born African-Caribbean adults under the age of 60 are in a formal marriage, compared with 60% of white adults. Moreover, this group is more likely than any other group to intermarry with whites. The number of mixed-race partnerships means that few African-Caribbean men and women are married to fellow African-Caribbeans; half of married or cohabiting British-born African-Caribbean men, and a third of women, are married to or living with white partners. Ali (2002) notes that such marriages result in inter-ethnic families and mixed-race (sometimes called 'dual heritage') children.

There is evidence that African-Caribbean communities have a higher proportion of one-parent families compared with white communities — over 50% of Caribbean families with children are one-parent families. There is a tradition in the African-Caribbean community of mothers choosing to live independently from their children's father. Only one-quarter of Caribbean children live with two black parents.

Berthoud (2003) suggests that the attitudes of young African-Caribbean women are characterised by **modern individualism** — they choose to bring up children alone because they are more likely to be employed than African-Caribbean men. Such women conclude rationally that African-Caribbean men are unreliable and are potentially a financial burden; they prefer therefore to be economically independent. Research indicates that these women are supported by an extended kinship network in their upbringing of children.

Berthoud found that the Pakistani and Bangladeshi communities are most likely to live in old-fashioned nuclear families, although about 33% of Asian families — mainly Sikhs and East African Asians — live in extended families. Berthoud argues that Asian family life is very traditional. Marriage is highly valued and there is little divorce. Marriage in Asian families — whether Muslim, Hindu or Sikh — is mainly arranged, and consequently there is little intermarriage with other religions or cultures.

Relationships between Asian parents and their children are also different from those that characterise white families. Ghuman (2003) notes that children tend to respect religious and cultural traditions, and that they feel a strong sense of duty to their families, especially to their elders. Many are happy to accept the tradition of arranged marriage as long as they can negotiate with their parents with regard to their future partner. South Asian families also feel a strong sense of duty and obligation to assist extended kin in economic and social ways. This is important, because Bangladeshi and Pakistani families in the UK are more likely to live in poverty compared with Indian and white families. Such obligations often extend to sending money to relatives abroad regularly and travelling overseas to nurse sick or dying relatives.

Class diversity

Traditional working-class families (where the husband works in long-established manual work such as mining or fishing) have tended to exhibit more segregated conjugal or domestic roles, and to maintain fairly widespread contact with kin and other members of the community. However, in the 1970s, the nature of working-class family life started to change and studies suggest that a new working class had emerged that was more privatised — i.e. not as open to kinship influences and more self-sufficient, as well as being more home-centred, with the couple sharing conjugal roles, especially childcare. Considerable time was now devoted by both parents to children and the upkeep of the home.

In recent years middle-class families have tended to be dual-career families, with both parents in full-time careers (home-centredness has been replaced by career-centredness). Such families are generally affluent and can indulge in exotic leisure pursuits. The parents are ambitious for their children but may have to rely on others, such as child minders, au pairs and preschool nurseries, to help in rearing their children because they are time-poor.

Middle-class families also tend to be smaller than working-class families. Working-class couples marry earlier and the birth of the first child occurs when they are relatively young. Other class differences might involve child-rearing practices — some sociologists suggest that middle-class parents are better at bringing up children, although this 'superiority' may be just a reflection of superior spending power and access to material resources.

Sexual diversity

More open attitudes regarding sexuality have led to an increase in the number of same-sex couples as well as families headed by two parents of the same sex. In 1999, the Law Lords ruled that a homosexual couple can be legally defined as a family. However, New Right commentators have suggested such family set-ups are unnatural and that children will either be under pressure to experiment with the lifestyles of their parents or will be bullied at school because of their parents' sexuality.

There have been a number of sociological studies of homosexual couples and children. These studies suggest that homosexual couples work harder at relationships in terms of commitment because they face so many external pressures and criticisms (for example, disapproval by other family members). Studies of children brought up in same-sex families show no significant effects in terms of gender identification or sexual orientation. For example, Gottman (1989) found that adult daughters of lesbian mothers were just as likely to be of a heterosexual inclination as the daughters of heterosexual mothers. Dunne (1997) argues that children brought up by homosexuals are more likely to be tolerant and see sharing and equality as important features of their relationships with others.

Regional diversity

Everslea and Bonnerjea (1982) showed that young upwardly mobile families tend to live in the 'sun belt' (the affluent southeast); older couples, widows and widowers retire to what they call the 'geriatric wards' of the south coast; more traditional working-class extended family structures are found in industrial areas suffering from economic decline; while the inner cities have greater concentrations of ethnic minority and single-parent families.

Explanations for family diversity

New Right sociologists often hark back to a **golden age** of family life when families were thought to involve a stable, secure, loving environment in which husbands and wives were strongly committed to each other for life and children were brought up in a disciplined fashion to respect their parents and social institutions such as the law.

Evaluation

- In the past, single parenthood was often disguised by mothers adopting their daughter's illegitimate children as their own.
- Young girls 'in trouble' (pregnant) were often made to undergo a 'shotgun wedding', whereby the young man concerned was forced by both sets of parents to marry the girl he made pregnant.

- Gay people often denied their sexuality and married someone of the opposite sex, thus living on the surface as a normal married couple.
- It is impossible to know how many 'empty shell' marriages there really were, whereby couples stayed together for the sake of the children or to keep up appearances.

Changes in society and social attitudes have contributed to more outward signs of family diversity. For example:

- **Changing moral values** around sexuality and increasing social acceptance of sex outside marriage have contributed to an increase in single mothers, cohabitation and same-sex couples.
- The **changing economic and social roles of women** in society have led to women demanding more equality with men within a relationship and being more confident and aspirational with regard to education and careers.
- The increased **feminisation of the labour force** has created dual-earner households and led to more equality in childcare arrangements.
- A number of writers, notably Connell (1995), have suggested that some men are experiencing a **crisis of masculinity** — they are unable to assert their status and masculine identity because of unemployment and the increasing success and assertiveness of women. This may lead to increased rates of suicide, drinking, family violence and often divorce among these men. This inevitably affects their relationships with their children. Other men have responded to women's increased career mobility by becoming **house-husbands**, staying at home with the children if their wives are able to earn more than they do.
- Greater rates of **immigration** after the Second World War and successive generations of ethnic minority groups born in the UK have increased family diversity both between and within ethnic groups. It is not uncommon, for instance, for some Asian women to become totally Westernised in relation to work and family life, while others retain a traditional approach.
- Further, there is increased evidence of **intermarriage** between different ethnic groups, with Britain having the highest rate of mixed marriages in Europe.
- **Greater sexual freedom and new reproductive technologies**, such as in vitro fertilisation (so-called test-tube babies) and surrogate motherhood, are affecting family diversity, as couples where one partner is infertile can now become parents together. Homosexual men may also donate sperm to lesbian women informally and in some family arrangements, they continue to have access to the offspring produced.

Postmodernists such as Stacey (1996) argue that family life is so diverse that it no longer makes sense to talk of the 'nuclear family'. Rather, a range of equally valid family forms exist. If we accept this observation, 'alternative' family structures such as lone-parent households and same-sex couples, as well as features such as serial relationships or childlessness should not be interpreted and labelled as 'problematic' or 'undesirable'. However, New Right sociologists argue that family diversity is exaggerated, and that the basic features of family life have remained largely unchanged for the majority of the population since the 1950s. Chester (1975) argues that most people experience the nuclear family at some time in their lives. New Right sociologists go as far as suggesting that, if properly supported, the nuclear family could solve many of the problems of modern societies, such as teenage pregnancy, truancy, educational underachievement, youth crime, street violence and drug misuse.

> ### Key concepts
>
> ideology of 'familism'; family values debates; nanny state; underclass; horizontal intra-generational ties; vertical intergenerational ties; class diversity; cultural diversity; cohort diversity; life-cycle diversity; regional diversity; changing moral values; changing role of women; economic changes; increased sexual freedom

Roles, responsibilities and relationships within the family

Relationships between men and women in the family

The symmetrical family

Young and Willmott (1973) argued that families were becoming, and would continue to become, more **symmetrical** — that is, the roles played by husband and wife within the family (conjugal roles) would become more 'equal'. Surveys investigating the distribution of housework and childcare tasks suggest that men today are more involved in domestic tasks than their fathers and grandfathers.

However, the Time Use Survey of 2005 carried out by Lader et al. found little sign that the traditional sexual division of labour in the home was changing. In 2005, women still spent more time than men cooking, washing up, cleaning, tidying, washing clothes and shopping. DIY and gardening tasks were still male dominated. Data from the British Household Panel Survey (2001) suggests that whatever the work–domestic set-up, women do more in the home than men. For example, when both spouses work full-time and even when the man is unemployed and his wife works, women put more hours into domestic labour than men.

The quantifiable evidence, therefore, indicates that women are still likely to experience a **dual burden** or **double shift** role, in that they are expected to be mainly responsible for the bulk of domestic tasks even if they hold down full-time jobs. They are also more likely than fathers to take time off work to look after a sick child. Dryden found that gender inequality in the distribution of housework and childcare was a constant source of irritation between couples and suggests this is a major cause of marital breakdown today.

Research by Gray (2006) suggests that fathers are keen to spend quality time with their children. In her study, fathers stressed that they wanted more time to get to know their children, to take them out, to help them with homework and to talk to them. However, she also found that many fathers are prevented by long working hours from spending quality time with their children and bonding effectively with them.

Decision-making

Edgell's (1980) survey of decision-making noted that while couples make some decisions together, especially those involving the children, men generally make the final decisions in regard to important issues such as finances (applying for a mortgage or how much to spend on a new car). Women rarely make decisions on their own — when they do they tend to focus on less important decisions such as buying new clothes for the children.

However, Gillian Leighton (1992) discovered that the power to make decisions changes when males become unemployed. In her study of professional couples, working wives often take over responsibility for bills and initiate cutbacks in spending.

Recent studies of conjugal roles

Recent research has focused upon other aspects of gender role inequality endured by women. DeVault (1991) points out that women do most of the **hidden work**, such as deciding what the family should have for dinner, making shopping lists, orchestrating the interaction around the dinner table and so on. Furthermore, women usually take responsibility for sending family birthday cards, buying presents etc. Duncombe and Marsden (1995) have highlighted the fact that women do most of the **emotion work**, empathising with and soothing children and partners in order to make their relationships work.

Relationships between children and parents

Evidence suggests that up until the middle of the twentieth century, children were treated as relatively insignificant, low status members of households who should be 'seen and not heard'. In middle-class and upper-class families, an authoritarian father figure would have little to do with parenting beyond imposing his decisions on his children's lives, leaving the rest to nannies, boarding school or their mother. In working-class families, children were seen as a financial burden until they were able to work and were made repeatedly aware of this fact by their parents.

Several developments have occurred which have qualitatively changed the relationship between parents and children in the family. Family life today is **child-centred** — parents see their children as the most significant members of the household. For example, a great deal of family activity is organised around the recreation and entertainment of children. The amount of time parents spend with their children has more than doubled since the 1960s. Parents discuss issues with their children, often valuing their opinions as those of equals. Children's welfare is now the major family priority, with no financial sacrifice seen as too great. There are several possible reasons for these developments:

- Families today are smaller, enabling parents to devote more time and attention, as well as financial resources, to each child.
- Parents, especially fathers, work a shorter working week than they did in the past and so have more leisure time which they can devote to their children.
- Greater affluence means that families have surplus money to spend on leisure with their children.
- Child abuse is much more tightly controlled by the state than it was in the past, with social workers actively intervening where children are not being looked after properly.
- A science of childcare — paediatrics — has grown in importance and many popular publications inform adults about good parenting skills.
- Childhood has been lengthened by legislation which increases the amount of time children spend in education. This prevents children from becoming financially independent and maintains the intense relationships between parents and children for longer. As one observer commented, 'Money isn't everything, but it sure keeps you in touch with your kids!'
- There is a broader range of options open to children as their lives also become more complex. These involve parents ferrying children to football matches or ballet lessons, for example. Parents frequently take an active interest in their children's leisure activities as a consequence.
- Largely unjustified fears and **moral panics** around the dangers of increased traffic or the threat from paedophiles has meant that children are less free to play outside unsupervised as they once used to. They thus spend more time indoors with their parents.

> **Evaluation**
> - The New Right suggest that there has been a 'loss of innocence' in childhood as children increasingly have access to formerly 'adult' material on issues such as death and sex via the mass media.
> - Children are less protected by their parents from the darker side of family life, as discussed on pages 31–32.

Sociological views of family roles and relationships

In relation to sociological views of changing roles and relationships, a number of theoretical justifications or critiques have been made either to challenge or support them.

Functionalism

Parsons and Bales (1955) argue that in the conventional (and desirable) nuclear family there are two complementary roles for the adult partners. The male plays the **instrumental role** of breadwinner and provider, and has the main contacts with the outside world through his employment, while the female plays the **expressive role** of nurturer and homemaker.

According to Parsons and Bales, these roles are based on the biological and evolutionary differences between males and females, and together provide the most suitable conditions for a stable family life and the primary socialisation of children. Parsons saw relationships between husbands and wives as complementary, with each contributing to the maintenance of the family in a qualitatively different way. Although dated, such thinking is still influential.

Feminism

Marxist feminists see family arrangements as beneficial to men and the capitalist class at the expense of women. They argue that the male workforce are able to endure their exploitation in the workplace because their wives 'repair' them emotionally and sexually at home so that they are fit for another day of exploitation at work. Benston (1972) argues that the family exploits women by expecting them to reproduce and rear the future workforce for free. Women provide free domestic labour without cost to capitalism (they are 'slaves of wage slaves').

Liberal feminists point out the ways in which men gain more from marriage than women. Married women have higher morbidity and earlier mortality than unmarried women, whereas married men are healthier and live longer than unmarried men. However, Liberal feminists also believe that women have made real progress in terms of equality in the family and that men are adapting to change, albeit rather more slowly than women.

Radical feminists see the family as an oppressive institution subjecting women to patriarchal power which, at its most extreme, is exhibited through domestic violence.

Evaluation

- These theories fail to explain why women's roles vary across different cultures. For example, the mother/housewife role does not exist in all societies.
- Feminism may also be guilty of devaluing the mother/housewife role as a 'second-class' role. For many women housework and childcare, like paid work, have real and positive meaning and men are often unable to gain the same level of satisfaction.
- Feminists may underestimate the degree of power that women actually enjoy. The fact that many women divorce their husbands indicates that they have the power to leave a relationship if they are unhappy with it.
- Catherine Hakim (1996) suggests that feminists underestimate women's ability to make rational choices. It is not patriarchy or men that are responsible for the position of women in families. She argues that women choose to give more commitment to family and children, and consequently they have less commitment to work than men.

Radical psychiatry

David Cooper (1972) suggested that the family overwhelms individuals, preventing them from thinking for themselves and realising their individual potential. This also serves capitalism, as the family produces well-behaved, obedient citizens who are easily manipulated by the ruling classes.

Edmund Leach (1967) argued that the family causes many psychological problems for children, such as schizophrenia and eating disorders, as it becomes increasingly isolated and inward-looking. Others are critical of the increasingly privatised nature of the nuclear family, where family privacy is respected to the extent that severe social problems are neglected (child abuse, domestic violence, drug and alcohol abuse).

The dark side of family life

Many writers have suggested that rather than being a warm and supportive environment, as functionalists and the New Right suggest, the family can be a hostile and dangerous place. The breakdown of marriage leading to divorce can often be the end result of bitter disputes and arguments between spouses. Rather than being harmonious institutions, families are often the sites of extreme violence and abuse. One in four murders takes place within the family on family members by family members. This is the darker side of family life.

Domestic violence

Dobash and Dobash concluded in 1980 that 25% of all serious assaults were committed by husbands on their wives. A survey on domestic violence, conducted in 1993, found that one in ten women had been victims of violence from their partners in the previous 12 months, yet only 22% of the attacks were reported to the police. Some surveys, however, have found the percentage of women attacked physically by a known male is over 30%.

Evaluation

- Official statistics on domestic violence are notoriously unreliable because this type of crime is often not recorded in crime statistics and many wives do not report their injuries to the police.
- Most women who do leave are forced to return home because of their economic dependence on their husbands.

Child abuse

Child abuse takes many forms (neglect, baby battering, physical attacks, sexual abuse etc.). Many writers have argued that families can literally drive children mad, causing mental disorders such as schizophrenia. In terms of physical abuse, there have been many cases of child murder and torture at the hands of parents or close relatives. The issue of disciplining children by smacking has been widely discussed and there has been pressure on policy-makers to make it illegal. Child sexual abuse came to prominence as a moral panic in the 1980s, when social workers in Cleveland removed several children from their families.

Feminists argue that the male sex drive is inherently dangerous for both women and children and that the extent of abuse by men in the family is widespread. Department of Health statistics for 1997 showed that nearly 14,000 children were on child protection registers in England alone.

- Many men regard the sexual or physical abuse of women and children as deviant and convicted abusers often have to be separated from other prisoners for their own protection.
- There is growing evidence of both physical and sexual abuse by women.

Non-feminist sociological approaches often link child abuse to social deprivation. Men who experience low status and self-esteem may be abusers in order to establish a sense of power over some aspect of their lives. Women who are lone parents may experience poverty and take their frustration out on their children. They are also more likely to have numerous sexual relationships with men who are not the fathers of their children, thus exposing them and their children to a greater risk of abuse.

Such explanations are based on the assumption that abuse only takes place in deprived families, whereas evidence suggests that this is not the case.

Demographic changes and their impact on family life

Family size

Women today are having fewer children compared with their mothers and grand-mothers. This is because they are starting a family at a later age and therefore produce fewer children. Furthermore, there has been a growth in childless couples. Women aged 30–34 are now more likely to give birth to their first child than women aged between 20 and 24. There are currently fewer than 60 births per 1,000 women of child-bearing age per annum compared with 117 at the start of the twentieth century. In the 1970s, fertility fell below the rate required to keep the population size stable (this ignores the effects of migration), and has remained below this level ever since.

There are a number of reasons for the fall in **fertility rate** and the increase in the average age of motherhood:
- the greater availability and choice of reliable contraception
- later marriage
- the increase in the proportion of women in higher education
- greater employment opportunities for women leading to an increased proportion in the labour market
- changes in women's perceptions of their role
- the high cost of raising children

Ageing population

People are living longer. This leads to greater numbers of elderly people, many of whom are unable to look after themselves. This may mean, in some cases, elderly relatives living with their children. In such cases, the burden of care generally falls upon female members of the household.

There are more elderly one-person households, sometimes supported by health visitors or living in warden-supervised accommodation. The number of one-person households over state pension age as a proportion of all households has gradually risen as life expectancy has increased and the population has aged. In 2005, 14% of all households were of this type. Women aged 65 and over were more likely than men to live alone because of their superior life expectancy and because they tended to marry men older than themselves. In 2005, 59% of women aged 75 and over were living alone.

Evidence suggests that many elderly people have regular contact with extended kin. Research by Phillipson et al. (1999) and O'Brien and Jones (1996) found that children and grandchildren saw their elderly relatives on a frequent basis, and the Office for National Statistics survey data collected in 2003 found that 61% of grandparents saw their grandchildren once a week. Many elderly relatives have started using new technology such as e-mail to keep in contact with their extended kin. Ross, Hill et al. (2006) found in their study that grandparents spoke positively about becoming and being a grandparent. When grandchildren are younger, time is spent together on outings and playing together, or with the grandparents teaching skills and providing childcare.

Key concepts

symmetrical family; women's dual burden role; women's double shift; hidden work; emotion work; child-centred; moral panic; instrumental and expressive role; dark side of family life; fertility rate; under-reporting and under-recording

Questions
&
Answers

This section of the guide provides you with eight questions on the topic of **The Family** in the style of the OCR examination.

The questions contain a range of grade A and grade C answers. It is important to note that the grade A responses are not 'model' answers. They are not the only possible answers to these questions nor are they necessarily the best. They merely represent one particular successful style; one that answers the question set and demonstrates the appropriate skills, especially using suitable concepts and studies, displaying a critical and evaluative awareness towards the material used and presenting a logically structured argument. Some grade-A responses are followed by a grade-C candidate's response. These are on the right track but, for various reasons, fail to score very high marks.

You must not, therefore, make the mistake of learning the A-grade responses parrot-fashion. Remember you have to be flexible and you have to be able to respond to the specific demands of a question. It would be quite possible, particularly in the answers to part (b), to take a different approach or to use different material, or even to come to a different conclusion, and still gain high marks.

A ninth question is provided which is not accompanied by a student answer. However, a plan of action is included and you should use this to write your own response. It is recommended that you spend some time revising the topic. You should answer the question under timed conditions with no notes.

Examiner's comments

The candidate's answers are accompanied by examiner's comments. These are preceded by the icon **℮** and indicate where credit is due. For the grade-A answers, the examiner shows you what it is that enables the candidate to score so highly. Particular attention is given to the candidate's use of the examinable skills; knowledge and understanding; interpretation and analysis and evaluation. For the grade-C answers, the examiner points out areas for improvement, specific problems and common errors. You are also invited to rewrite the answer in order to gain higher marks and some pointers are given to show you how you might do this.

Reminder of mark allocations

Each structured question totals 50 marks, composed of 17 marks in part (a) for AO1 (knowledge and understanding), and in part (b) 10 marks for AO1 (knowledge and understanding), 13 marks for AO2(a) (interpretation and application) and 10 marks for AO2(b) (evaluation and analysis).

Families; households; family diversity

(a) Identify and explain *two* ways in which families differ from households.   (17 marks)

(b) Outline and evaluate the view that families are now so diverse that the idea of the 'normal' nuclear family no longer applies.   (33 marks)

Total: 50 marks

Answer to question 1: grade-A candidate

> The first part (a) below illustrates how candidates can end up with a grade significantly below their ability by doing relatively badly in part (a) of the question.

(a) The first way that a family differs from a household is that members of a family are either related through marriage or by blood. Members of a family usually consist of members of different sexes and they usually contain children. Within a family there is some form of support, whether it is financial or emotional, provided for members. A household just contains members who live together. As one sociologist said, 'all families at some time live as households but not all households are families'. For example, students who live together may consider themselves to be a family as they are close and perhaps share money etc. but officially they would be classed as a household.

> There are too many features of a family mentioned here. The candidate has not sufficiently addressed the command words 'Identify and explain *two* ways…'. The difference between any feature and a household needs drawing out, as the candidate leaves it implicit. The question merely requires demonstration of AO1, knowledge and understanding, so the evaluative comments cannot be rewarded. This is a common mistake in part (a) answers, where candidates waste a considerable amount of time addressing skills not required in the answers to this part.

The other way in which families differ from households is the way in which they are defined. Murdock invented a definition in 1949 which was quite narrow and did not include many groups which today we would class as families. The definition includes one partner of each sex, which would exclude homosexuals. In contemporary society a homosexual couple with children would be known as a same-sex family. This means that some people who would previously have been classed as a household would now be called a family. A family and a household could be the same or different, depending upon your definition.

> Again, these are very interesting evaluative comments which demonstrate good awareness but the question does not require the candidate to demonstrate this and so no marks can be awarded. The candidate scores 6 out of 17 for identifying

relatedness but then explaining the difference between household and family poorly, and making only brief reference to support. Despite the writer having obvious potential as a grade-A candidate, this part (a) answer only scores an E.   Mark: 6/17

Alternative grade-A part (a) answer

A family comprises blood and other relatives, over two or more generations, not necessarily in shared residence. For example, the children may have grown up and left home. A household must involve common residence. Members of households may or may not be related — they may be same-aged adults, that is, not a range of generations.

> This answer in itself is almost enough for grade-A marks as it contains two clear differences — relatedness (family); relatedness or not (household); common residence or not (family); common residence (household). There is even a possible third difference: multi-generational (family); same generational or multi-generational (household). The last sentence needs to be developed further to provide a fuller explanation of this difference.

Also, families tend to have mutual obligations and emotional ties. It is expected that parents will provide for their children out of love and duty. Households need not involve members in providing for each other. It is likely that some activity will be shared, such as meals, but non-family household members are much more independent than family household members. An example of a non-family household is a group of students sharing a house.

> This second paragraph describes a clear difference between family and household — a high level of mutual dependency (family) versus a low one (household). Note that the candidate understands clearly the idea that families can also be households by using the phrase 'non-family household'. This answer scores full marks.
> Mark: 17/17

(b) The 'normal' nuclear family is a very stereotypical image. It has also been referred to as a 'cereal packet norm'. Anne Oakley states that the 'normal' nuclear family consists of a mother, father and their dependent children. The image of a happy nuclear family, in which the male provides for his family materially while the female provides domestically and emotionally, is seen in a large number of places, one of them being the mass media. The nuclear family is seen as the ideal family by many. Politicians see this as the ideal family structure, as do functionalists, who believe that everybody will benefit from it.

> Implicit reference to family ideology is being made here. The candidate has taken on board the emphasis of the question, adopting an evaluative tone from the start. It is a good approach to adopt a sceptical stance to the view expressed. A common weakness to part (b) questions is for candidates to present a one-sided justification for the view expressed. Bear in mind that questions will always express a view that can be challenged. This answer would benefit from some examples of media representations or politicians' views.

In contemporary society, there are many different family forms, with the nuclear family being just one. Lone parents are a new, increasingly accepted family structure. There are two different types: those who have never married, and those who were once married but became widowed or divorced. Lone parents are seen as bad by structural functionalists and political parties. New Labour aims to help lone parents help themselves through the 'welfare to work' scheme, where they are guaranteed more money through eventual paid employment. New Right sociologists, in contrast, blame all of society's evils on lone parents and use them as scapegoats. They aim to get rid of lone parents by reducing benefits and forcing them into employment.

🖉 Again, while locating the view of the normality of the nuclear family with the New Right and functionalists, this answer needs some examples to back up the points made. In what way are lone parents seen as bad? Some mention of Murray (1990) and the underclass thesis would be relevant here.

Divorce is viewed as bad by politicians and functionalists, although if we look at statistics of people who divorce we see that most remarry. This shows that it is not the idea of marriage that people dislike, only that they have married the wrong person. This in a way can be seen as good for society, as people will be careful to choose the right partner next time and then live in a desirable family structure. People who remarry live in what is known as a reconstituted family, where there are perhaps step-relations. This could be beneficial to members, as the children will have more role models and more people there for the process of socialisation.

🖉 This section lacks focus. Reference to the continuing popularity of marriage could be used to show the persistence of the nuclear family as a perceived ideal. It is not clear why reference to marriage is included here. Although obviously relevant as an example of diversity, it is also not clear why reconstituted families are referred to and the alleged benefits are asserted but unsupported by evidence.

As the sociologist Chester says, the nuclear family has changed from conventional to neo-conventional. The family has just adapted. Changes have been minor as most people live in a nuclear family at some time in their lives.

🖉 This is a key point but poorly expressed. An examiner would give it the benefit of the doubt; however, you should make sure that you express crucial arguments as clearly as you can. 'Chester argues that the nuclear family has not declined in significance. He refers to a neo-conventional family, which involves two parents, a small number of children and long-term commitment. But unlike the traditional or "normal" nuclear family, it often involves women working part-time outside the home. The nuclear family has merely adapted to changes in women's roles.'

It is not just the case that family structures have become more diverse, many older family forms such as the extended family and the traditional nuclear family have re-emerged because of immigration to Britain. In some Asian families, for example, extended family living is common as, because of racism and language barriers, family members both live and work together in family businesses. In a recent article in the *Guardian* newspaper it was reported that Asians are more likely to live as traditional nuclear families than any other group.

> This is a very strong paragraph which has an evaluative tone and uses contemporary examples well. Be wary, however, of using the term 'Asians'. This covers a wide range of ethnic subdivisions which have diverse family forms. In this instance the article refers to Pakistani families.

Even though the government and other agencies are beginning to accept other family forms, the ideal of the nuclear family is still pushed.

> Examples are needed, such as the fact that child benefit is paid directly to mothers, therefore seeing them as sole care-givers; most social housing is designed for a small nuclear family of four members.

In contemporary society many different family structures are starting to be accepted, whereas previously they were thought of as deviant. Overall though, the nuclear family still seems to be the type of family people aim for. Throughout a person's life an individual may move through different family structures, so that at some time they may live as a nuclear family and at other times not. Postmodernists use this idea when they talk about family pathways. In fact, postmodernists argue that it doesn't any longer make sense to talk about 'the family'; we should instead talk about 'families'. By this they mean that there are lots of family forms and all of them should be seen as equal and none deviant.

> It is good to see some mention of postmodern thinking on the family. This topic is a key area where postmodernists have challenged conservative views and the candidate demonstrates a good level of understanding of their contribution in this context.

So to go back to the original question, functionalists say the nuclear family is still the most important. Others say that diversity is to be tolerated but the nuclear family should be more recognised, while postmodernists say it no longer makes sense to talk about the nuclear family as so many other forms exist which are just as good.

> This is a good, albeit brief, conclusion that summarises the main arguments in the answer.

> Overall, although this is a rather long and rambling answer, the candidate gets there in the end. The candidate loses focus at times and the answer is a little thin in terms of evidence, but a good level of overall understanding is demonstrated and the answer has an evaluative tone. As you are required to answer two questions on the paper, however, you must make sure that you divide your time equally. Rather than exceed the 45-minute limit for each answer, it would be better to conclude in note form. This candidate is either a fast writer or they ran out of time to do their second question justice.

Marks: AO1 7/10; AO2(a) 8/13; AO2(b) 8/10 Total 23/33

Total for question including first part (a): 29/50

Total for question including second part (a): 40/50

Answer to question 1: grade-C candidate

(a) Two ways in which families differ from households: firstly we need to define family. Family is a group of people who live in the same household which consists of father, mother and their children, whereas a household is just a group of people living together. A family differs from a household as a household can contain people who are not related, for example it could be a group of friends. A family helps each other out emotionally and financially. They stick together and solve family problems; households can be separate.

> *e* This is a rather confused and poorly expressed response which suggests that the candidate is aware of differences but cannot identify and explain them clearly. The first sentence recognises implicitly that family members must be related, whereas household members need not be, but the identification is weak. A second difference is also weakly identified — that families tend to have stronger obligations towards one another. You should aim to write two brief paragraphs which clearly identify the two factors and which offer a clear explanation of each using relevant examples to back up your points. **Mark: 8/17**

(b) The idea of the 'normal' nuclear family no longer applies as families are now so diverse. Some sociologists believe that the family is not dying. Rather, it is going through changes. This is blamed on an increase in divorce, quadrupling of teenage pregnancies contributing to a general increase in single parents. Almost a third of all children now live in reconstituted families which basically means having a step-family. Reconstituted families are families in which a man or woman has gone through divorce or been widowed and has remarried, bringing with them children from the previous relationship.

Reconstituted families have the highest rates of divorce. The New Right also claim that more people are divorcing as divorce is now more easily available and also serial monogamy is being blamed. This means that a couple goes through a series of relationships following divorce then remarriage.

> *e* This is a very rushed response and far too much ground is being covered without sufficient depth. There is some confusion over what is being asked by the question and it smacks of a rehearsed answer in view of the lack of focus. Some potentially good points are lost here. If the candidate's basic point here is in favour of the view, they need to say so. Always make it clear which position your points relate to, otherwise you give the impression that you lack understanding and you could lose marks.

Almost 70% of all families need state intervention in the form of income support or family credit. Britain has the highest rate of teenage pregnancy in Europe after Denmark. This resulted in the Child Support Agency being set up, where absent fathers are traced and made to contribute financially. However, it costs more to run than the money it gets from absent fathers and women resent being dependent on men they have ended a relationship with. Also, many men are in new families and paying for their existing children affects their new family.

> It is not really clear why the points above are made. Implicitly, the candidate seems to be saying that family diversity is supported by the state, thus providing further evidence in support of the view posited in the question. Again, the candidate needs to refer to the view constantly in order to focus the response more on the question.

As well as single-parent families and reconstituted families, there are also some same-sex families where the homosexual couple (usually women) can adopt children or have an artificial insemination donor. The Rappaports wrote about other types of diversity including cohort diversity, where one group of families have good luck because times are better whereas another family suffer problems, such as in the 1980s when the mines closed. That cohort had hard times while everyone else did OK. Differences in families' organisation can be seen with ethnic groups who often live as extended families. West Indians have more single parents than anyone else. So you can see that the family is now very diverse and the nuclear family does seem to have died a bit. But it is still very important and we see the cornflake packet family, which is nuclear, every day on television.

> This is a much more explicit paragraph which provides a good range of sociological evidence for the view expressed in the question. The candidate also briefly evaluates at the end, bringing us back to the question.

> Overall, this is a fairly typical, middle-of-the-road answer which is mostly assertive of the view expressed in the question. There is a general lack of clarity here and there and occasional lapses in focus. It is also a little brief. Nonetheless, the candidate does demonstrate a sound knowledge of family diversity and of an ideological dimension to the debate. There is a fairly good range of evidence and some pertinent evaluative comment.

Marks: AO1 6/10; AO2(a) 7/13; AO2(b) 5/10 Total 18/33

Total for question: 26/50

Q2

Marriage and divorce

(a) **Identify and explain *two* reasons for increases in the divorce rate up to the mid-1980s.** (17 marks)

(b) **Outline and evaluate the view that a rise in the divorce rate does not necessarily indicate dissatisfaction with the institution of marriage.** (33 marks)

Total: 50 marks

Answer to question 2: grade-A candidate

(a) The first reason concerns legal changes making it easier for divorces to be granted, although these may have also been brought about by changing social attitudes. The single most influential law was the Divorce Law Reform Act of 1969, implemented in 1971. It removed having to prove grounds such as adultery or cruelty and simply required the marriage to have irretrievably broken down. If both partners agreed, they could divorce after 2 years' separation. If only one agreed, then 5 years' separation was necessary.

> ⧉ This answer offers a very clear identification and full explanation. There is more than enough here for full marks.

Secondly, the influence of feminist ideas meant that women were no longer expected to put up with a bad marriage rather than be 'on the shelf'. Women's rights to personal happiness and fulfilment within marriage came to be seen as basic (women are the main petitioners for divorce, with about seven of every ten divorce decrees granted to women). Thornes and Collard showed that women still expect more from marriage than men and so are more easily dissatisfied, although in recent years the divorce rate has leveled out.

> ⧉ Again, the answer is clearly identified and fully explained. Note how the candidate gives equal weight to each reason, identifying each clearly and fully explaining both with excellent examples.   Mark: 17/17

(b) If we take divorce statistics at face value, there is no doubt that people appear to take marriage less seriously than they did 30 or 40 years ago. Even people who got married in church and took vows saying that they would remain married 'until death us do part' get divorced, sometimes after only a short period of marriage. After 1984 people could get divorced after being married for only a year. Changes in the divorce laws come about following major changes in society. For example, the 1971 Act coincided with the rise of feminism and a lot of women were declaring their dissatisfaction with the perceived sexism of their husbands. However, the New Right has made divorce less straightforward again and since 1996 there have been additional requirements to seek counseling, arrange childcare and financial provision for children and allow a period for reflection and reconciliation. If

reconciliation fails within a year, divorce is allowed. So, again, the New Right felt that things had gone too far. Still, it is now accepted that genuinely ill-matched or unhappy people should not be made to stay married to each other.

🖉 This is a very good introduction which shows an understanding of what the question is asking. It demonstrates detailed knowledge of contemporary changes in the divorce laws which are linked to changes in the wider society.

However, this is not the whole picture. Although the divorce rate is high, about three in five marriages will not end in divorce, a fact that is often forgotten. In addition, many divorced people will in fact remarry, showing that it is not marriage they are disenchanted with, but marriage to a particular person. More than two out of every five marriages are second marriages for one or both of the partners.

🖉 This is a useful paragraph, which shows that a simple look at the divorce rate does not give the whole picture. Analysis/evaluation skills are evident.

According to *Social Trends*, despite the growth in cohabitation, 'marriage is still the usual partnership between men and women'. Having said this, it is true that the actual number of marriages taking place is falling. There are now just over 330,000 marriages a year, including remarriages — the lowest figure this century. However, the statistics suggest that the trend in rising divorces is leveling out, and that the rate is stabilising. There are a growing number of people who choose not to marry at all, the so-called 'singletons'. They may be disenchanted with the institution of marriage, though we would need research to tell us if this were true. If they are disenchanted, it is obviously not linked to the divorce rate but is a separate phenomenon. It is also possible that some people — for example battered wives — are disenchanted with marriage but they do not necessarily get divorced for a number of reasons, such as religion, finance or for the sake of the children.

🖉 A good paragraph which shows balance between the arguments and evidence being put forward and demonstrates all skill areas. It is useful to show that you know and understand the different points of view and interpretations of the evidence.

Overall, we have had a period of rising divorces and falling marriages which, on the face of it, would seem to suggest that the statement in the question is true. However, it could be argued that the fact that people divorce rather than remain in an unhappy marriage means that the institution of marriage is more, not less, important to them. We also have to take into account the high rate of remarriage; these people are obviously not disenchanted with marriage. A growing number of people are marrying more than twice, so we have a situation of serial monogamy. It has to be concluded, then, that a rise in the divorce rate does not necessarily mean that people are disenchanted with the institution of marriage.

🖉 This conclusion draws together the main evidence and interprets it according to the requirements of the question. The final sentence shows clearly the conclusion reached by the candidate. It should be remembered that it is not always possible to do this; the arguments and evidence surrounding some topics are so complex that it is difficult to come to a firm conclusion. This is quite acceptable, provided that all the main points of view have been aired and the difficulty or impossibility of reaching a simple conclusion has been acknowledged.

☑ Overall, this is a well-focused answer, showing good evidence of the skills. More could have been said by the candidate about the impact of cultural norms and attitudes on people's views of marriage and divorce, showing how difficult it is to reach a simple conclusion on the link between divorce and ideas about marriage.

Marks: AO1 8/10; AO2(a) 10/13; AO2(b) 8/10 Total 26/33

Total for question: 43/50

Answer to question 2: grade-C candidate

(a) The first reason is the spread of feminist views and women's lib so women won't stay trapped in an unhappy marriage and are more likely to have the money to set up on their own. The second reason is changes in the law.

☑ The first part of the answer identifies a reason (the spread of feminist views) and gives a brief explanation of how this is linked to the rise in the divorce rate (3+3 marks awarded), but the second part simply identifies a factor (changes in the law) and so cannot gain any marks for explanation (2 marks awarded).   Mark: 8/17

(b) In most societies, divorce is on the increase, and Britain has one of the highest rates of divorce. The number of divorces has been going up since the 1970s, when the law changed to make it easier. Nowadays people don't necessarily expect a marriage to be 'until death do us part', so the idea of divorce has almost become a part of marriage. About one in three marriages end in divorce.

☑ There is some relevant knowledge and understanding here, with information about rising divorce rates and a hint about changing attitudes to marriage. Is it strictly true to say that in 'most' societies divorce is on the increase? It largely depends on which part of the world and what kind of society you have in mind. While it is legitimate to start a question such as this with some 'background' information about divorce, this only becomes truly relevant if the information is picked up and carried through the rest of the answer. In this case, the discussion of the rise in the divorce rate has to be linked to the question of whether or not this is evidence of disenchantment with the institution of marriage.

One of the reasons for this is changes in women's attitudes. With the rise of feminism and women's lib, women have come to realise that they don't have to put up with an unhappy marriage if they don't want to. Also, if you have seen your parents get divorced, it will seem more normal to you. Divorce is also talked about a lot more, and lots of personalities and characters in the soaps are divorced or talking about getting divorced, so it is very much a part of society.

📝 This paragraph gives some reasons why the divorce rate might have risen, but these are fairly simplistic and are not developed.

Feminists such as Barnard have shown that marriage is better for men than women, and a lot of married women become ill, so they must think 'Why should I put up with this?' This has led to a big increase in the number of lone-parent families, and the New Right believe that this is one of the causes of crime in society, while others say that it brings a lot of people into poverty.

📝 A very brief mention is made of the feminist interpretation of health differences between married women and married men, but this is only weakly linked to the discussion. Lone-parent families, crime and poverty are not relevant to the question.

Quite a lot of people still do get married, and there is media interest in weddings. Also, some divorced people get married again (serial monogamy). There are a lot of couples who cohabit, and who therefore are as good as married, especially as in a lot of cases the law now treats them as though they were man and wife. Also, the age of marriage is rising so a lot of people in their late twenties and thirties who could be thought of as not intending to marry, may still marry when they get older, once they have made a career or managed to save up for a proper wedding, which can cost over £10,000 these days.

📝 The answer here touches on 'marriage', the other part of the question. The comments about the number of marriages in society, the media's interest in weddings and the remarriage of divorced people are all potentially relevant but none is allowed to further the discussion. However, some good points are made about the impact of cohabitation (should this be treated differently from 'marriage'?) and people who delay marriage rather than refrain from it. The point about the law treating cohabitees as though 'they were man and wife' is not true.

So it is hard to say whether people are disenchanted with the institution of marriage. One of the main pieces of evidence that marriage as an institution is still valued is that most divorcees remarry and often bring their children to the new relationship to create step-families. People even get married several times these days, like Pamela Anderson, and so experience serial monogamy. On the face of the evidence, therefore, marriage is still going quite strong.

📝 The candidate rounds off with a pretty good conclusion which uses some central concepts in this debate. It is a pity that they weren't introduced earlier; they appear as an afterthought rather than as a central argument.

📝 Overall, the candidate shows a reasonable knowledge and understanding of the topic, although the relevance of some of the material to the topic is not made explicit. There is some limited analysis and evaluation, for example about cohabitation and delayed marriage. At 400 words, the answer as a whole is rather brief.

Marks: AO1 6/10; AO2(a) 7/13; AO2(b) 6/10 Total 19/33

Total for question: 27/50

Functionalist views on the nuclear family; Marxist and feminist critiques; dark side of family life

(a) Identify and explain *two* ways in which the nuclear family benefits its members. (17 marks)

(b) Outline and evaluate the view that the nuclear family is bad for its members. (33 marks)

Total: 50 marks

Answer to question 3: grade-A candidate

(a) According to functionalists such as Parsons, the family has two irreducible functions which are good for its members. First, stabilisation of adult personalities — couples ease the burden of work and social life for each other, relieving frustration and tension, and enabling them to operate in society in a purposeful and rational manner.

🖉 This shows clear identification. It is good to locate a question theoretically where you can, in this case functionalism. The candidate might also have referred to the New Right. However, this response demonstrates good understanding. The explanation is clear and concise.

Secondly, functionalists say that the family is good for its members because it enables effective socialisation of the young to take place. This occurs through the expressive role of the mother who socialises her offspring emotionally and the instrumental role of the father as a material provider, socialising the children into the adult roles required by the wider society. Boys and girls have appropriate role models and discipline, preparing them for adult roles.

🖉 This answer offers very clear identification and explanation.　　Mark: 17/17

(b) The view that the family is bad for its members is one held by a wide range of social commentators from all of the sociological perspectives. Even some functionalists such as Vogel and Bell argue that adults use children as an emotional scapegoat. This means that tensions and conflicts existing between parents are projected onto the children. So the parents offload their problems onto their children, relieving tension, but the children are left emotionally disturbed. One sociologist studied societies with extended family networks, which supported members by providing emotional support and practical help. This led him to believe that the nuclear family is too isolated and could blow like an overloaded electrical circuit because it keeps all of its problems to itself.

> **✍** This is a sophisticated introduction which demonstrates a very good grasp of the debate from the outset. It is better to avoid saying 'a sociologist said'. Try to attribute an idea, if not to a person, then to a perspective.

Radical psychiatrists go even further and suggest that the family is so damaging that it can cause severe psychological problems such as schizophrenia. Laing felt that most behaviour problems were the result of essentially mad family life. Other radical psychiatrists added a Marxist angle to this by suggesting that the family is an ideological conditioning device (Cooper?), which makes individuals more easily manipulated by capitalists, as it removes their individual creativity.

> **✍** If you think you know who said something, have the strength of your convictions and say so. Nonetheless, this is a strong paragraph which provides a good link to the discussion of Marxism which follows.

Marxists argue that the nuclear family is not supposed to be good for its members. It provides a more flexible and mobile workforce and is an excellent unit of consumption. Each family needs its own car, cooker, washing machine, fridge, television etc. when such items could easily be shared under other living arrangements. Then of course fewer goods would be sold. Advertisers target the nuclear family ideal, which they present as an ideology of familism, sometimes called the 'cereal packet image' of the family.

> **✍** A good paragraph with plenty of potentially relevant points. It loses focus a little, as it does not make it clear why the nuclear family is bad for its members. After all, capitalists would argue that we all have a much better standard of living in this consumer society. The candidate might have highlighted how consumer fetishism (obsession with the latest thing) is a false need which robs individuals of the means to acquire true consciousness about what they need to do to change society into a fairer, less exploitative, state of being.

A number of feminist sociologists including Oakley, Ansley, Delphy and Leonard have pointed to the number of ways that women are disadvantaged in the family, especially wives and mothers. Feminists believe that we live in a patriarchal society — that is, a society where men have most of the power — and this gives men power in all situations, including within the family.

> **✍** This is a strong paragraph which includes the names of some relevant feminist sociologists, and demonstrates a good understanding. The important concept of 'patriarchal society' is introduced, with an explanation showing that it is clearly understood.

Although this is no longer the case, the feminist argument is that women are still exploited within the family. Oakley's research showed the unequal division of domestic labour within a household, and much more recent studies than hers have shown that, in spite of most women now having paid employment, they still spend much longer on housework and childcare than their partners. Being a wife/mother and a worker leads to a 'dual role' for women in the family, but Dunscombe and Marsden have gone further and said that we should also include the caring and nurturing role (what Ansley has called being the 'takers of shit') and therefore women can be said to have a 'triple shift'.

🖉 The response is neatly brought back to the present by the phrase 'although this is no longer the case', and by the candidate pointing out that feminists believe that exploitation is still taking place. Oakley's study is used well, the main point being made without spending time describing the study in detail, and with an important comment showing understanding of the fact that it is now quite dated. There is some good use of relevant concepts — 'division of domestic labour', 'dual role' and 'triple shift' — together with further reference to relevant sociologists.

Exploitation at work means that most women earn less than men, but even when they are a big contributor to the household finances, their earnings are often seen as supplementing the man's, with the man still being seen as the main bread-winner. Taking time out to have babies and look after them, at least for a while, also has a bad effect on women's careers, putting them way behind men in the promotion stakes. Women with young children often have to fit their work around childcare commitments, leading many of them to work part-time. Also, men still tend to take the major family decisions. For example, it is usually the man's job that determines where the family will live.

🖉 The reference to work and women's earnings is tied closely to the question of women's disadvantages arising from the family, avoiding the danger of going off the point and simply talking about unequal pay at work. The issue of male power in decision-making is also raised, though not pursued.

Lastly, studies have shown that married women have poorer health than single women, probably as a result of all the extra work they do, and the strain of having to be the comforter and supporter of all the other members of the family. There is also the sad fact that many women are the victims of domestic violence, and recent reports show that this is actually on the increase. Children too are often victims of abuse.

🖉 A further area of disadvantage is raised, that of health, with some suggestions to explain why this should be so. Reference is also made to the important issue of domestic violence, and knowledge of recent information on this topic is shown.

The family, therefore, appears to be a bad place to be as far as its members are concerned, unless one adopts the feminist position which sees men as benefiting enormously from it. However, many recent feminists, for example Germaine Greer writing in the late 1990s, as well as C. Hakim, point out that women may choose the wife/mother role as it is a very fulfiling one. Traditional roles for men leave them cut off from their children all day and almost totally in the event of divorce, as they rarely gain custody. It is also true that many find family life extremely rewarding and couples unable to have children will go to extreme lengths to try to become a family. So, in conclusion, some families may be bad for some members but there is as much evidence to suggest that the family is also beneficial.

📝 The answer is brought to a conclusion with some evaluation of the debate, including the use of further information to act as a form of counter-balance to the feminist arguments and the evidence that has previously been discussed. It is partic-ularly refreshing to see some reference to recent feminist accounts. The answer is concluded with a reference to the original question.

📝 Overall, this is a very good answer which stays firmly focused on the question and shows a good knowledge and understanding of the topic. Appropriate use is made of relevant sociological concepts, and there are pertinent references to feminist sociologists. Some reference could have been made to different types of feminism. The answer is quite long, and some students might find that they are unable to write as much as this in the time provided. Despite the occasional flaw, this answer is better than one might expect to see at AS. The level of theoretical discussion in particular shows sophistication more typical of A-level. Consequently, considering it was written by a notional 17-year-old under exam conditions it would be awarded full marks.

📝 Note that the question could have been answered from a completely different angle by focusing upon the so-called 'dark side' of family life, as the C-grade answer below demonstrates.

Marks: AO1 10; AO2(a) 13; AO2(b) 10 Total 33/33

Total for question: 50/50

Answer to question 3: grade-C candidate.

(a) The nuclear family is good for its members because it provides a way for couples to satisfy each others' needs. Couples can have regular sex together without going beyond the relationship and catching a disease.

📝 It is not clear how satisfaction of sexual needs is necessarily provided within the nuclear family. The emphasis on sex in isolation does not take account of social factors such as sex outside the family, for example adultery causing marital instability or confusing issues of inheritance, economic support etc. A factor is identified here but is poorly explained.

Also, the family provides members with love and support, mothers especially dealing with emotional problems and preventing loneliness.

> ✏️ The candidate does not focus specifically on the nuclear family, instead providing an example (love and support) that could be generalised to all family forms. Hence both explanation and identification are weak. **Mark: 8/17**

(b) The family isn't always a cosy and friendly place to be. Most murders occur within the family. Divorce is commonplace and so this suggests that for the couple at least, the nuclear family is not a good place to be. Feminists have long argued that the nuclear family is bad for women. They argue that the husband gets a lot more out of it as married men live longer than unmarried men and vice versa for women.

> ✏️ Although this has a rather journalistic style, the candidate introduces some negative aspects of family life, thus immediately focusing the discussion upon the question. The final point is potentially a good one and it should have been further developed. It doesn't really make sense as it stands, although the candidate would have been given the benefit of the doubt.

Radical feminists even argue that all men are rapists and men have for centuries raped their wives. This was made illegal in 1971. The rape of women in the family is only part of a whole cycle of abuse. The husband and wife sociologists Dobash and Dobash wrote about the extent of domestic violence in the home. They found that one in four women had been beaten by their husbands yet hardly any ever went to the police. And if they did, the police just saw it as 'a domestic' and didn't do anything. This probably means that a lot more women are actually victims of domestic violence but they don't see any point in reporting it. Also, the women have nowhere to go as they can't support themselves financially. There are now a lot more refuges and the social will support women in extreme danger.

> ✏️ Be careful with dates. If you are not sure, do not include them. Rape within marriage was recognised as illegal in 1991. There are lots of strong evaluative points here which are worth developing. Avoid colloquialisms; I presume 'the social' is a reference to Social Security.

Just living normally in a family is actually bad for women. Not only do they work a lot harder and longer than men, doing housework even if they work full time, but if they have a job, they usually have to take time off if their child is sick and when they get pregnant they lose out because it is their career that suffers.

> ✏️ This is rather assertive in tone and needs some evidence in the form of sociological studies to back it up. An example is required to show how careers may suffer, such as having to adopt flexible working hours around childcare, which no longer fits the needs of a high-powered job.

Finally what about the kids? The nuclear family is obviously bad for a lot of them too. Children suffer physical abuse, even murder, at the hands of close relatives. Victoria Climbie was recently beaten, tortured and eventually murdered by her aunt and her boyfriend, which was a kind of nuclear family because they were looking after her (or not) instead of her parents. If a lot of other relatives were around, like in the days of the extended family, this kind of thing would be less likely to happen.

This makes a good point and evaluative comment about the extended family providing support and informal social control. However, the point deserves further development. Using contemporary examples demonstrates to the examiner that you are able to apply your sociological thinking to your own experience.

Of course, the nuclear family is not all bad, otherwise we would see through the happy smiling faces that beam out at us every day from cereal packets and our television sets. Most people identify a positive feeling with the nuclear family or else it wouldn't be used to sell products. Husbands and wives and children have much closer relationships than they did in the past and the family is now more child-centred, which can only be good for the kids.

A very good evaluative comment which brings us back to the original question.

So in conclusion, the nuclear family may be bad in some cases but generally most people think it is good or else it wouldn't be so popular. Mind you, it isn't as popular as it seems because only 40% of people live in one. Still, they could live in one in the future.

The last couple of points come across as something of an afterthought. These points were certainly worth developing as they are important. The fact that the nuclear family is a minority family form, taken as a snapshot of all families, could indicate that there is indeed something wrong with it as far as the experience of its members is concerned. If, on the other hand, most people have experienced it, may again or are yet to experience it as Chester argues, then it must also be perceived positively.

Overall, there are quite a lot of sound arguments presented, with a generally evaluative tone throughout. The answer suffers from being over-assertive and a little one-sided, as well as lacking the necessary depth to achieve a top grade.

Marks: AO1 6/10; AO2(a) 7/13; AO2(b) 6/10 Total 19/33

Total for question: 27/50

question 4

Single person households; family diversity

(a) Identify and explain *two* reasons for the growth in single person households in the contemporary UK. (17 marks)

(b) Outline and evaluate the view that the family is in decline in the contemporary UK. (33 marks)

Total: 50 marks

Answer to question 4: grade-A candidate

(a) One reason is that there are more women living alone due to the increased economic independence of women; women are no longer 'a husband away from poverty'. Career women can earn high wages, enabling them to afford a mortgage of their own. Also there has been a rise in the number of divorced or separated people who have not formed another partnership yet and so live either in the marital home on their own or who have moved into separate accommodation, usually rented, until the financial arrangements between former partners become finalised.

    The candidate writes rather more than is really necessary. Both reasons are clearly identified but explanations are a little anecdotal.   Mark: 13/17

(b) This view can be taken in two ways — either that today families are no longer as influential on the lives of the individuals in them in a positive way, or that families are becoming less common due to demographic and other factors.

    This is an interesting introduction which demonstrates to the examiner immediately that the candidate is thinking sociologically in addressing the actual question, rather than embarking on a prepared answer.

The former view is primarily proposed by New Right thinkers and some functionalists who suggest that socialisation in modern society is becoming less effective because of trends such as increasing divorce and the lack of a father in many one-parent families. They go on to argue that this is contributing to social problems, such as increased delinquency and educational underachievement. Fewer marriages and increased cohabitation, as well as the growth in single-person households are also said to indicate a decline in family life.

    The candidate gives a clear exposition of the New Right position.

However, ideas about the nature of family life in the past often underestimate the problems families faced back then. The New Right often harks back to a 'golden age' of family life, when families were thought to be stable and happy, with both parents together and committed to one another for life and doting on their children. However, single parenthood was much more common than is supposed, as it was often disguised by mothers adopting their daughters' illegitimate children as their own. Young girls 'in trouble'(pregnant) were often made to undergo a 'shotgun wedding', whereby the young man concerned was forced by both sets of parents to marry the girl he made pregnant. Gay people were often forced to deny their sexuality and marry someone of the opposite sex, living as a normal married couple on the surface but having homosexual relationships on the side. It is impossible also to know how many empty-shell marriages there really were — where couples stayed together for the sake of the children or to keep up appearances. In other words, the tendencies in family life that may lead to social problems are not all new. It may be that the family in the past was actually much worse, as there were fewer opportunities to seek alternative arrangements or escape from its negative aspects.

This is a very strong critique of the New Right position. The examples given are all relevant. Although there is an anecdotal tendency and lack of reference to studies or empirical evidence, the candidate uses concepts confidently.

Postmodernists have highlighted how family life today has become more fragmented and consumer-orientated, such that family members strive to assert their identities not through their class or ethnicity but through consumption. They therefore tend to 'do their own thing' rather than share activities such as mealtimes and leisure pursuits. However, this does not mean that families were cohesive and happy together in the past, when 'children should be seen and not heard' or children saw shared activity as a chore.

This is a relevant paragraph but the link to the preceding one is not made sufficiently clear. It needs a linking sentence such as 'While family life in the past may have been more fragmented than is often suggested by the New Right...'. The candidate's train of thought is a little confused and the evaluation needed to be clearer. This could be picked up by the candidate on rereading their answer and the sentence suggested above slotted in as superscript.

The other argument to consider in opposition to this view is that the family may be in decline if we accept the cereal packet view as the norm. Families are very diverse today and, as postmodernists suggest, all forms may be said to be equally authentic and worthwhile. Also, any comment on family life is merely a snapshot, as people go through various stages of family life, being in nuclear families, in single person households, as part of a reconstituted family and perhaps by experiencing several arrangements more than once.

This argument might have been developed further by giving examples of a typical family life cycle.

This brings me to the second aspect of the view that demographic changes are causing a decline in family living. It is true that some (particularly middle-class) women are choosing career and singlehood over family and motherhood. However, working-class and ethnic minority families show no signs of decline. Foster has shown in her book *Villains* that extended families are common among the white working class and are mutually dependant in the contemporary UK. Ethnic minority communities vary in the family arrangements they make but extended families are strong among Sikh families (horizontally — brothers, sisters, aunts, uncles, cousins mutually supportive) and Bangladeshi families (vertically extended — several generations together). Chinese and Greek families are often extended. The nuclear family is strong among Pakistanis. So many immigrant groups contribute to this family form's persistence in the UK. However, recent immigrants from Eastern Europe have tended to be young singletons, which may counter these trends.

This is a relevant paragraph which demonstrates that the candidate is staying focused as they have returned to their original interpretation of the question. It is rather rushed, suggesting perhaps that they were running out of time and so some of the points made are underdeveloped. Always make sure you pace yourself and cover the plan for the essay evenly.

While families may have changed they have not declined significantly. In any case, we have no way of proving that the family was more cohesive and influential in the past.

Although this is a little brief, it is good practice to summarise your key arguments in conclusion. Overall, this is a strong response which includes a lot of examples and concepts rather than studies or statistical evidence. However, the theoretical emphasis on New Right or postmodern thinking could have been supplemented by some mention of Marxist and feminist thinking, which argues that the family is very influential, often to the detriment of all or some of its members.

Marks: AO1 9/10; AO2(a) 10/13; AO2(b) 8/10 Total 27/33

Total for question 40/50

Answer to question 4: grade-C candidate

(a) There has been a growth of 'young singletons', including young people who may be in a relationship but who choose to live alone.

Weak identification and explanation. 'Young singletons' is a phrase which the candidate has remembered but it is not clear here that it is fully understood. Quite why there has been such a growth is not made clear (for instance later marriage plans, more affluence, more opportunities for leisure which would be inhibited by cohabitation or marriage).

There are also more old people who lose a partner (usually the women) so this makes more single-person households.

📝 This is a weak identification and explanation. Again, why there are more old people is not made clear (for instance improved healthcare, changes in fertility rate etc.).

Mark: 6/17

(b) The idea that the family is in decline has been around for some time. As well as the nuclear family, which was the norm after the war until about the mid-1970s, there are a lot of single-parent families, reconstituted families which are often larger than the norm because of there being children from two marriages. There are same-sex couples, comprised of two women who have had children by artificial means. However, ethnic minorities also have different family forms. Many African-Caribbean women are single parents and some Asians still live as extended families.

📝 The candidate writes a rather confused opening. The examples given are not necessarily illustrative of decline, rather of diversity. The candidate does not locate the view either in New Right or functionalist thinking and so there is no clear position to support or challenge.

But one reason the family may be in decline is that the government doesn't provide enough housing any more to enable its different forms to live as they would choose. The government should provide larger council houses for extended families. Same-sex families should have the same rights to benefits as heterosexuals. The government should recognise that nuclear families are now the minority and not just cater for them.

Some policy does recognise diversity, such as single parents being given a council flat. Some people — New Rights — say that this encourages young girls to get pregnant but I think this is a media hype and most don't do it for this reason. So the government needs to recognise more family diversity, as we now live in a postmodern society where anything goes and that also applies to the family.

📝 This could have been quite a strong paragraph if the candidate had been clearer about why the points it contains were being made. For example, that family diversity, which might demonstrate flourishing family life in a range of alternative forms, is being stifled by a lack of recognition of this through government policy and provision.

The other point is that there are more problems caused by the crisis over masculinity. Many men have lost their jobs and so feel emasculated. Such men may turn to alcohol and even suicide. An unemployed man is 11 times more likely to commit suicide than an employed one. In addition, this could cause more family violence. Dobash and Dobash have shown that one in four women are victims of domestic violence, although this cuts across all social classes and ethnic groups.

🖉 This could have been better expressed. It comes across as assertive and unsubstantiated.

This does not mean that things are necessarily in decline though domestic violence was very common in the past. It is certainly true that family life is much more uncertain than it used to be. Marriage is less common and people are marrying later. There are more teenage pregnancies and there are more gay people living the life of young singletons but many do cohabit and have children through artificial means or adoption. Extended families are less common but there is a lot of evidence to show that the family is alive and well in the contemporary UK.

🖉 This answer lacks structure and loses focus. There doesn't seem to be much of a plan in evidence. The candidate clutches at straws at times and it is not really clear why certain points are included. They could be relevant but the arguments are not clearly expressed and application is poor, as there is little attempt at linking the evidence to specific sociological arguments. Nonetheless, there is some sound knowledge (though limited understanding) and some attempts at quite sophisticated evaluation.

Marks: AO1 6/10; AO2(a) 7/13; AO2(b) 6/10 Total 19/33

Total for question: 25/50

Demographic change; women's roles

(a) Identify and explain *two* recent demographic changes and the ways in which they have affected family life. (17 marks)

(b) Outline and evaluate the view that changes in women's role in society have had a major impact upon family life. (33 marks)

Total: 50 marks

Answer to question 5: grade-A candidate

(a) Demographic changes mean changes in the structure of the population. One demographic change is that the birth rate has gone down because women go to work more than they used to and have children later. The impact that this has on family life is that families are more child-centred as parents have fewer children to focus on and they have more resources available to each child. They may, for example, be able to afford expensive holidays abroad etc.

✐ The first demographic change is clearly identified. It was not necessary to give any reasons for the change though. The impact on family life is clearly explained.

A second demographic change is that there is now an ageing population as older people live longer and fewer children are being born. The impact of this on family life is that families may have to take in older relatives and look after them. The burden of care usually falls upon women. Otherwise the elderly may have to sell their homes to pay for care, which means their children have less inheritance.

✐ Again, the demographic change is clearly identified and this time the reasons offered clarify the meaning of 'ageing population'. The impact on family life is clearly explained and concluding remarks demonstrate excellent knowledge of related issues. Both changes were well identified and their impact explained. Balance is important in part (a). It is a common error for candidates to over-elaborate one of the two points and to gain few marks for the other. This candidate addressed both well and would gain full marks for AO1 knowledge and understanding.

Mark: 17/17

(b) Before assessing the view above, I will first outline some of the changes in women's roles which have occurred. Women are now virtually equal to men in the workplace. They do not on average earn as much but they are catching up. Girls are out-performing boys in the education system and there are many women with high levels of power and status. It is no longer the case that women are expected to become a housewife once married nor is it the case that women adopt a subordinate position to men. Women are now assertive in their working and emotional relationships and have high expectations.

📝 A good start which immediately focuses the answer on the question asked. It also shows that the candidate is aware of the wider social context within which the discussion is located.

Much of this has been achieved through the efforts of feminists in the 1970s, who were able to demonstrate how exploited and oppressed women were. They raised women's consciousness and put pressure on men to change society into a more equal one.

📝 This brief historical note shows that changes in women's roles were hard won and relatively recent. Fortunately, this point is kept very brief and avoids the tendency to discuss at length something that is only marginally relevant to the question. Unless a historical perspective is obviously required by the question, it is better to stick to contemporary issues and material, for example the last 20 years.

Most women now go to work and many delay childbirth or even choose to remain childless. Functionalists and the New Right fear that children may be suffering maternal deprivation and becoming inappropriately socialised. This could lead, they argue, to increased deviance. According to Parsons, the mother plays the emotional and central expressive role in the family. She is naturally inclined towards looking after the needs of family members, while her husband is the instrumental leader, destined to provide for the family's material needs. Women, however, now have higher expectations, which also means that they are much more demanding in marriage. This is one reason for the increase in the divorce rate since the 1970s. Women account for over 70% of petitioners for divorce. In terms of negative impact on family life, the New Right argue that women working has created 'latch key kids', that is, children who look after themselves after school, perhaps ignoring homework, watching inappropriate videos or getting into trouble without adult supervision. More divorce also creates more lone-parent families, which New Right thinkers such as Murray consider dysfunctional, with children being prone to educational underachievement and crime.

📝 This is a very full paragraph with no wasted points. The functionalist position is clearly presented and contextualised. It is a common error for weaker students to present theoretical arguments in a list-like, isolated way. Here several examples are given of the alleged negativity of women working. However, the candidate also uses the functionalist arguments sociologically, by suggesting that traditional expectations of women may have created dissatisfaction and further fuelled the rising divorce rate.

There are, however, many positive arguments. For one thing, families are more affluent due to women's additional income and so have a better standard of living. Women now provide positive role models for their daughters. Indeed, one feminist

initiative persists today. The 'Take Your Daughter To Work Campaign' encourages women to do just that once a year in order for their daughters to see that the workplace is a normal progression route for girls. Girls' self-esteem is much higher than it once was due to the vast numbers of high-achieving female role models. While exaggerated to some extent by the media, 'Girl Power' is evident everywhere you look.

> The candidate gives some good contemporary examples of positive outcomes from women's greater involvement in the workplace. Although theoretical evidence is not essential, some reference to recent feminist ideas would give the response more weight.

One of the key changes to affect family life as a result of women's changing roles is the nature of conjugal relationships. Young and Willmott showed that men were taking more of an active role in the home and predicted that families would become symmetrical in this respect. At one time, men had virtually no responsibility for domestic work and childcare. This has undoubtedly changed but symmetry is, even in the twenty-first century, still a long way off. Oakley showed that Young and Willmott were exaggerating the extent of male involvement and that women still did the majority of domestic tasks. Some feminists have argued that women do a double shift of work plus housework while others, such as Dunscombe and Marsden, suggest that they even do a triple shift, adding nurturing and caring. They call this 'emotion work'. Whether men do share housework more equally or not, recent writers have suggested that there is more to it. Edgell demonstrated how decision-making in the family is unequal, with men making all the important decisions such as when to move house and women making the minor ones like how to decorate it. DeVault points out that women also do most of the hidden work such as deciding what the family should have for dinner, making shopping lists, making the family meal a social experience etc. Also women usually take responsibility for sending family birthday cards and buying presents for other family members.

> This is a good overview of the domestic labour debate which has been kept focused on the question. There is the danger that candidates take comfort in familiar territory and write about what they know at great length, deviating from the question asked in the process. It is nice to see reference to some contemporary material and no mention of 1950s sociology, such as Elizabeth Bott.

In conclusion, it can be argued that changes in women's roles have had a major impact on family life, increasing affluence, affecting the motivation of girls, socialising males to be more aware of females as equals and increasing the involvement of men in childcare and household tasks. However, many feminists argue that family life has not really changed that much, as the nuclear family is still oppressive to women.

The question is brought to a conclusion with a brief summary of the issues raised by the question and an evaluative comment, thus reaffirming the overall focus on the question.

This is not the best grade-A answer possible but the candidate uses what they know quite well. Remember every mark counts towards the overall AS grade and ultimately the full A-level. So you can compensate for a weak performance in one module with a good performance in another.

Marks: AO1 8/10; AO2(a) 9/13; AO2(b) 7/10 Total 24/33

Total for question: 41/50

Changing economic and domestic roles of men and women; changing relationships within the family

(a) Identify and explain *two* ways in which family life may be influenced by recent changes in work patterns. (17 marks)

(b) Outline and evaluate the view that relationships within the family are becoming more equal. (33 marks)

Total: 50 marks

Answer to question 6: grade-A candidate

(a) One way in which family life is affected by recent changes in work patterns is...

> The examiner knows what the question is. Don't bother writing it out in full as you will waste valuable time.

...due to the fact that more and more women are entering employment. Parsons said that a woman's natural role was that of an expressive leader who socialised the children and looked after her husband and the house. The entire way the family functions may change if women are employed. For example, children may have to go to child minders who care for several children and so primary socialisation may be affected. As women become more financially independent and less reliant on their husbands, this could lead to divorce.

> The candidate alludes to several effects on family life here but none is well explained.

The opposite effect has been happening for some men. Many men are being made redundant due to the decline in manual work, traditionally done by men, and middle-class redundancies in the service sector. Women have been more successful in gaining employment than men in recent years. Some sociologists such as Connell go so far as to say that this is causing a crisis for masculinity. For the ex-manual workers research shows high levels of depression and even suicide and family instability, with women being resentful breadwinners while the men do very little. But in the case of some middle-class men, the outcome has been more positive with the development of house-husbands. They recognise their wives' superior earning power — which they see as positive — and stay at home and get to know their children.

✏️ This is a very strong response demonstrating that the candidate has really engaged with this aspect of the course to develop a strong understanding and some real sociological insight. Responses like these are a pleasure to read.   Mark: 12/17

(b) In contemporary society, it can be seen that relationships within the family are indeed becoming more equal. In this essay I intend to show that this is the case to some extent for women and men, as well as between parents and children.

✏️ The candidate unpacks the question and clarifies what they understand it to require of them. There are several approaches to this question, perhaps focusing on the domestic labour debate solely, or the shift to child-centredness. This dual approach may be forgiven for a certain degree of superficiality in order to provide a broad overview of the issues, for example depth may have to be sacrificed for breadth.

To take women and men first, more women are employed and so financially independent. This means that they are no longer reliant on their husbands. This, therefore, has created more equality between the genders because women are no longer seen as subordinate and men as dominant.

✏️ While this may be true, it is rather assertive and some evidence is really needed to back it up — perhaps recent feminist ideas or statistics showing women's increased mobility. On the other hand, a considerable amount of feminist material would show that power differences persist.

Willmott and Young conducted a study in Bethnal Green in East London in the 1950s which showed quite diverse roles between men and women. The women had close contact with their family, their mothers in particular, whereas the men did not. The women made the community and the extended family much closer. As one old lady in an ITV documentary commented, 'We was all one', meaning that everybody in the community shared their lives together. However, relationships within the family changed as people moved away due to slum clearance and in search of work as local industries declined. Young and Willmott found that the ex-eastenders in Greenleigh lost contact with their extended families and they became known as isolated or privatised nuclear families. Leisure activities became more home-based and involved gardening or watching television rather than going to the pub. Children got more attention as families also became more child-centred. Also conjugal roles became more similar, leading Willmott and Young to conclude in the 1970s that the family was becoming symmetrical in terms of roles. Although many feminists argue that this is not really the case and that women still take on most of the responsibility for domestic roles, relationships have undoubtedly changed. Few men adopt a patriarchal position as the head of the household these days and there is even evidence of some role reversal with, as I said above, the development of house-husbands.

question

e An informed broad-brush approach is effectively employed here which contextu-
alises well the reasons for changes in male and female roles within the family and
community. The idea of equal but different is implicit in the discussion of roles in
the 1950s, when women played a pivotal role in maintaining family relationships.
There is scope for some evaluation here with the shift to privatised living initially
causing a sense of isolation and loss of purpose and fulfilment for many women.
This is evidenced by the increased use of tranquillisers — so-called 'mother's little
helpers' — throughout the 1960s and early 1970s.

The socialisation of boys and girls is also less segregated. It is still true that children
have a clear sense of gender identity by the age of 4 or 5 and may choose different
toys. But some effort has been made to reduce the level of overt sexism in
children's reading books and most parents encourage both genders to take an
active part in helping around the house. This is not always the case, however, in
certain ethnic groups. Several Turkish female friends of mine complain that their
brothers are much more free than they are and do nothing around the home,
expecting them or their mothers to run around after them. Fairly traditional gender
roles persist among some Asian groups also.

e There is nothing wrong with using pertinent and relevant empirical examples from
one's own experience but be careful not to generalise. Again, the question is lapsing
into assertion and would benefit from some sociological references, for example
the work of McRobbie.

To conclude I will now discuss another area of increasing equality — that is,
between parents and children. Families are now much more child-centred and
children are no longer 'seen but not heard'. Parents idolise their children and spend
a lot of time and money on them. You need only look at a shopping mall on a
Saturday afternoon to see evidence of this. Parents value their offspring's opinion
and often seek their advice on a range of issues. Children no longer live in fear of
their parents to the extent that they once did. Postmodernists argue that rules
imposed on children have been replaced by negotiation with them and children
have as much right to make demands of their parents these days.

e The candidate makes some good points that show a high level of conceptual
awareness. There is some attempt to introduce sociological evidence but the
answer still suffers from being somewhat assertive.

However, one should not overlook the fact that many children are victims of abuse
and some parents exert unreasonable levels of power over them.

e This is a good evaluative point. Always try to counter the overall argument
presented in a paragraph by an assessment of it at the end.

So, in conclusion, relationships within the family have become much more equal,
both between men and women and parents and children, but some abuses of
power still exist. Some men mostly abuse their wives with domestic violence, as
Dobash and Dobash have shown, or physically and sexually abuse their children.

✍ A bit rushed towards the end but it is good practice to revisit the question. The candidate obviously thought of Dobash and Dobash at the last minute, which is a shame as this could have been a better developed evaluative point earlier on.

✍ Overall, this is a comprehensive overview of the main issues showing a very good level of knowledge and understanding of the key issues, as well as consistent and sustained evaluation. While the extent of sociological evidence is rather narrow, the candidate does compensate for this by using contemporary examples, some of which are well drawn from their own experience.

Marks: AO1 8/10; AO2(a) 8/13; AO2(b) 7/10 Total 23/33

Total for question: 35/50

Question 7

Family and social change; nuclear and extended families

(a) Identify and explain **two** differences between nuclear and extended families. **(17 marks)**

(b) Outline and evaluate the view that the extended family no longer plays a significant role in family life in contemporary Britain. **(33 marks)**

Total: 50 marks

Answer to question 7: grade-A candidate

(a) Nuclear families are two generation, parents and children, while extended families can be three-generation — a vertically extended family of grandparents, parents, children. Nuclear families are geographically mobile whereas extended families live in the same area for generations.

> The first difference needs to be explained more to gain full marks. It is possible for a couple to have an older child at university living at home and a new baby if, for example, the woman was 20 when her first child was born and 40 at the birth of the second. This would still be a nuclear family. The second answer is well identified but again needs a fuller explanation. Mark: 8/17

(b) According to Willmott, there is a new type of kinship. Social changes have led to the extended family becoming much less important than it was in the past, such as in the 1950s and 1960s, when Willmott and Young did their research into family life in Bethnal Green. It has been replaced by a privatised nuclear family, which functionalists argue better meets the needs of modern industrial societies.

> This is a good introduction which shows knowledge of the classic Bethnal Green research and makes an evaluative point regarding the link to the functionalist view.

The Bethnal Green research showed a working-class community where there was not much geographical mobility, with most people living in the same small area in which they had grown up, and where there was frequent day-to-day contact between family members, especially daughters and their mothers. The families were highly 'mum-centred' (matrifocal), and few of the women went out to work, leaving them time to visit and go shopping with their mothers and sisters.

> This demonstrates further relevant knowledge of the kind of extended family relationship found by Willmott and Young, though it would have been unwise to write much more on this, as the focus of the question is on the situation now.

It is true that there have been many important social changes that have had an effect on the frequency of face-to-face contact between people and their wider kin. One of these is geographical mobility. When Willmott and Young studied families who had moved from Bethnal Green to the suburb of Greenleigh, which was only 33 miles away, they found that the families had become more home-centred and privatised, and that the wives didn't have such regular contact with their mothers, and had developed a more intimate relationship with their husbands.

✍ This answer makes good use of appropriate sociological concepts.

However, how the evidence is interpreted depends on what definition of 'extended family' is being used. If it means regular, daily, face-to-face contact, then it is probably true to say that the extended family has declined in importance. Should we use this definition, though? Fiona Devine went back in the early 1990s and looked at car workers and their families in Luton, revisiting a study first carried out by Goldthorpe and Lockwood. Devine argued that the amount of privatisation in the family had been exaggerated, as her findings showed that most couples did keep in regular contact with their kin, not only their parents, but also their siblings. Such contact has been made easier with the spread of car ownership and telephones. Finch and Mason, in their study of families in Manchester, also found that people still relied heavily on kin for a range of help and advice, for example financial help, emotional support and looking after children.

Janet Foster in her study *Villains*, which was of an East London community in the 1990s, showed that the classic extended family is even still in evidence with generations of relatives living close by and providing significant material and emotional support to each other. Willmott's own later research, using the number of contacts between relatives rather than just face-to-face meetings, showed that most people keep up contacts, with a high proportion still seeing at least one relative at least once a week. He notes the emergence of a dispersed extended family. Here members live some distance apart but keep in fairly regular contact, perhaps once a week by car, telephone and public transport. While not dependent on each other, they do rely on each other on an occasional basis. The growing use of e-mails and the internet, especially among older people, means that it is even easier for people to keep in touch with relatives, even when they live thousands of miles away.

✍ These paragraphs have an evaluative tone throughout, and use appropriate research to illustrate the point that the extended family is still relevant, although the definition of the term has been modified. The candidate might have referred to Litwak's work on the modified extended family (a coalition of nuclear families who maintain a degree of contact and support). The candidate makes good use of studies and demonstrates sound knowledge of appropriate concepts.

It is also true that a number of families, especially the women in them, look after elderly relatives in some way. The policy of 'care in the community' has meant an

increase in the number of elderly people who have to be looked after outside care institutions, and for many of them it has meant care in, or by, the family. Such responsibilities are some of the factors that lead many women to work part time rather than full time.

The candidate provides further evidence that challenges the view expressed in the question.

Among some Asian ethnic minority groups, the extended family plays a very important role, and such families are likely to have three generations living under one roof, or at least to have regular face-to-face contact.

This recognises different cultural norms and practices among different groups in society.

There is also evidence that extended kinship ties are still important among the upper class in their attempt to maintain their wealth and privilege. They use marriage and family connections to maintain their class boundaries and to keep out non-elite persons.

Another problem facing sociologists is that many of the views about the so-called 'golden age of the family' are actually myths and not based on hard evidence. It is very difficult to prove that close contacts with relatives and giving and receiving help among relatives was actually that much greater in the past than it is today.

The candidate makes further important evaluative points.

The view that the extended family no longer plays a significant role in family life in modern Britain does not seem to be supported by sociological evidence. Relatives are still a major source of help for most people, and contact is maintained, even though this might not be frequent face-to-face contact. What has happened is that our definition of 'extended family' has become modified.

This brief conclusion relates to the question and summarises the main points made throughout the answer.

The brevity of part (a) has enabled the candidate to write more extensively than normally expected. This is a very good answer; it stays focused on the question, shows good skills, especially evaluation, and a range of appropriate knowledge. The candidate scores maximum marks.

Marks: AO1 10/10; AO2(a) 13/13; AO2(b) 10/10 Total 33/33

Total for question: 41/50

Lone parenthood; divorce; dark side of family life

(a) Identify and explain *two* reasons for the growth in lone-parent households.

(17 marks)

(b) Outline and evaluate the view that reported increases in divorce, child abuse and domestic violence indicate that family life in contemporary Britain is dying.

(33 marks)

Total: 50 marks

Answer to question 8: grade-C candidate

(a) There are lots of reasons for the increase in lone-parent households. One is higher divorce which means a third of people who marry get divorced. Another reason is that teenagers have sex younger these days and they usually get given a flat which, with just them and their baby in it, is a lone-parent household.

> This answer is far too brief. The first reason is correctly identified as divorce but no explanation or evidence is given as to why this may cause lone parenthood. The candidate needed to point out that custody of children is given to one parent (usually the mother) and the non-care-giving parent is expected to provide some financial support which, with state benefits, enables divorced women to look after their children independently. The second reason is assertive and unsubstantiated. Most teenage mothers (only 3% of all lone parents) live with their families. An ESRC study showed that only one in ten live in social housing 6 months after the birth of their babies. The candidate would only therefore get a couple of marks for identifying a rather weak reason: 3 marks for identifying divorce; 2 marks for teenage pregnancy and 1 mark for assertive explanation. **Mark: 6/17**

(b) Over the last few years there has been a big increase in divorce. Couples used to stay together for the sake of the children in so-called empty nest marriages. Now, because of less disapproval from other people, they just get divorced. Also the law has changed to make it easier to get divorced. The Legal Aid Act of 1949 meant that even poor people could afford to get divorced.

> This paragraph focuses immediately on the question, but the evidence presented lacks depth and accuracy as well as being dated. The candidate means 'empty-shell marriages' and reference to divorce law reform before 1971 is more historical than sociological.

Also, there are now a lot more paedophiles around and because of them being encouraged via the internet, many fathers are sexually abusing their children. Society is becoming more violent and children and women are becoming victims in the home.

📝 An over-assertive tone is used here. It is better to start a sentence with evidence. If you are referring to a popular view it should be attributed as such. Better candidates might have picked up on the word 'reported' in the question and addressed the extent to which perceptions of increased sexual abuse may be socially constructed.

Studies have shown that up to one in three women are physically abused by their husbands and even raped, but this is now illegal. Dobash and Dobash did a study which showed that one in four women are victims of physical abuse. Children are also getting abused and the charity Childline takes thousands of calls a week.

📝 Obvious and relevant knowledge is presented here but it is lacking in sufficient depth to demonstrate full understanding. Again, the opportunity for the candidate to make evaluative comments about the relationship between child abuse statistics and greater opportunities to report is missed.

Some politicians call for a 'back to basics' approach to the family as they feel that family life is in chaos, with too many lone parents and problems of delinquency, as well as people taking advantage of the welfare state. So the view has a lot going for it but there are a lot of other arguments to consider. Some argue that a far too rosy picture of the family in the past is painted and no golden age really existed. Families were 'empty nest' and there was a lot more poverty. We also don't know how much domestic violence there was in the past and women nowadays are more likely to come forward and they have refuges to go to. The same thing is true about child abuse. There was no Childline then so nobody knew about it. As for divorce, some feminist said it is far better to live with one loving parent than two who argue all the time. So, it is not possible to say for sure whether the family is dying or not. Even though the divorce rate is very high, it's slowed down and when people do divorce they tend to remarry anyway. There is a lot more family diversity about these days: lone parents, same-sex (gay) couples, step-families, so you could say that no, the family isn't dying it is merely changing.

📝 There is a lot of good relevant material here with plenty of evaluation. The knowledge of key issues is implicit rather than fully spelled out, for example the New Right position. Also, the interpretation and analysis lacks depth. Nonetheless, this is a good paragraph written under exam conditions by a 17-year-old having completed 1 year of sociology.

📝 Overall, this answer is a little brief at 400 words; you should aim to write at least 500 words in 33 minutes. The answer is well focused on the question and quite wide-ranging, but is rather rushed and superficial, lacking detail. The grade C is just achieved with the help of a fairly good part (b).

Marks: AO1 6/10; AO2(a) 7/13; AO2(b) 7/10 Total 20/33

Total for question: 26/50

Family change and diversity

(a) Identify and explain two examples of how family life may be influenced by ethnicity. (17 marks)

(b) Outline and evaluate the view that a dominant family type no longer exists in the contemporary UK. (33 marks)

Total: 50 marks

Individual task

This question is for you to try yourself. You should spend some time researching suitable material and making notes, and then try to write the answer in 50 minutes — the time you are allowed in the examination. Below are a few pointers in order to help you get on the right track.

Part (a) question

With all part (a) questions you need to demonstrate knowledge and understanding:

- Students are expected to spend about 15 minutes on this part (half to three-quarters of a side of writing).
- Good answers must be balanced, addressing both factors evenly.
- Explanations should include evidence and examples, either from studies, statistics or personal experience.

With this question you need to look at examples of family diversity among different ethnic groups. Make sure that you don't generalise. 'Asians', for example, is a term which would include a wide range of different ethnicities such as Bangladeshi, Indian, Pakistani and Chinese or religions such as Muslim, Hindu, Sikh, Buddhist and even Christian. The full range of family diversity can be found among them. You might also look at examples of family life among Greek, Jewish and West Indian communities. Note that the question refers to family 'life' and so would allow you to go beyond a discussion of family structure to discuss the differing customs within each ethnic household that relate to family living.

Part (b) question

- Candidates are expected to spend about 30 minutes on this part (2 or 3 sides of writing).
- The view expressed will be attributable theoretically, ideologically, or sociologically. This means that the ideas expressed by the view come from somewhere, for example Marxists, the New Right, feminists, functionalists, postmodernists. You should therefore demonstrate awareness of this and of various counter-arguments and positions.
- Top answers will provide evidence of a range of types for or against the view. There will be some reference to a theory or studies and/or you will include statistics or examples from everyday experience.

- Clear conclusions will be formed after balanced consideration of evidence — you must consider evidence or opinions against the view. Always bear in mind that the view is not merely presented for you to support. In this case, consider the New Right view — the ideology of familism — as well as postmodern views. You may also consider family diversity in terms of conjugal role diversity, kinship diversity, ethnic or class diversity and life-cycle diversity.

Revising the essay

When you have finished, draw a line under your answer. Then refer to your notes and the relevant pages in this guide and write in a different colour pen additional points of relevance that you left out. As this material did not readily spring to mind first time round, reread it and ask people to test you on it.

The finished essay

Once you have been through the revision process above, try to rewrite your essay in 45 minutes. Now ask your teacher to mark it. Do this with other questions in this guide.